W9-BWI-469

A Poetic Equation:

Books by Margaret Walker

For My People
Jubilee
Prophets for a New Day
October Journey
How I Wrote Jubilee

Books by Nikki Giovanni

Black Feeling, Black Talk/Black Judgement
Re: Creation
Spin a Soft Black Song (for children)
Gemini
My House
A Dialogue (with James Baldwin)
Ego Tripping and Other Poems (for children)

Record Albums
Truth Is On Its Way
Like A Ripple On A Pond

A Poetic Equation: Conversations Between

NIKKI GIOVANNI

and

MARGARET WALKER

Howard University Press

Washington, D. C.   1974

LIBRARY OF CONGRESS CATALOGING IN PUBLICATION DATA

Giovanni, Nikki.
    A poetic equation.
      1. Giovanni, Nikki.   2. Walker, Margaret, 1915-
II.   Title.
PS3557.155Z52   815'.06   73-85494
ISBN 0-88258-003-5

All photographs for this book were taken by Jill Krementz, except the following for pages 3, 19, 25, 39, and 52 by Mr. N. Alfred Handy III.

For my dear Alex, my lover, sweetheart, best boy-friend, and best of all my ever-loving husband for more than thirty years!

M. W.

To Sister Althea, Theresa, Flora and Ida—for all the same reasons.

N. G.

Preface

Nikki Giovanni and Margaret Walker would naturally gravitate toward one another, being women, black, and writers with that particular temperament of the poet.

In October of 1972 both were invited to read at the Paul Laurence Dunbar Centennial at the University of Dayton, Dayton, Ohio—the home of the early poet. The first evening of the program featured several writers reading from the distinguished poet's work. Margaret Walker read "The Party" replete with the "folk talk," humor, and warmth that much of Dunbar's work renders. She captured the spirit of the work, and I think of the man, as only Margaret can— her eyes twinkling, her lips shaping the contours of his verses, the rise and fall of her voice signaling the poem's special meanings. Much of the audience, which gave her a standing ovation, had probably heard her read her own poems in that same extraordinary manner, among them the classic "For My People"—a classic which is not only her signature poem, but the signature poem of a people. When drawn into the heart of her words, one cannot help but feel that exhilarating sense which is only felt in the presence of a very special person.

Nikki Giovanni read the next day to an already full auditorium which practically doubled by the time she was due to appear. Upon her arrival and all through the reading there was an electricity that pulsed through the crowd of mostly young students responding to the heightened sense of presence that emanates from her five-foot frame. To watch her read her poetry is quite an experience. She has that rare ability to give what she takes in: to complete that very special circuit of communication. For Nikki can seize the moment: read the kind of poems (she read many of her new love poems) and talk about the kind of things that her audience, in a particular place and at a particular time, wants and needs to hear. Another standing ovation ensued and it was after her reading that I went toward the stage to say hello—and left Dayton with a book idea.

Over a cup of coffee and in between excited questions from students who had followed her to the canteen, Nikki and I talked about our mutual friend, Margaret. Nikki suggested that I do a conversation book with Margaret and that she would be more than willing to supply an introduction if I wanted one. We both agreed how rich a book like that would be by this grand lady whose career had also included associations with many of the writers and artists of the thirties, forties and fifties, including Richard Wright, Langston Hughes, and Melvin Tolson, among many others.

After thinking this over for a few moments I said, "Why don't *you* do the book with Margaret?"

"I don't want you to think I was looking for a job."

"O.K., but what do you say?"

"If Margaret will agree to it, I think it would be great."

That evening I had dinner with Margaret Walker and proposed the idea. She said, "I think it would be interesting, I'd love to." So, a book was born. And when I started thinking about the "parents" of this child I was intrigued with the possibilities. Margaret Walker had decided to sow her seeds in the South (her home is Jackson, Mississippi) after finding the northern soil of Chicago and New York interesting, but not the kind of stuff from which her roots are grown. She is a woman who reflects the values of a generation of blacks steeped in scholarship (and proud of it), who experienced the Depression, World War II, the rise of the American Communist Party and McCarthyism, and a racial perspective which had its own particular kind of radical and conservative aspects.

And Nikki Giovanni, a virtual embodiment of the sixties and seventies: controversial, in constant physical and mental movement; not only unafraid to explore the dichotomies of the times and of herself, but determined to lay them bare. Her sensibility thrives in an urban world, and she has shored up her life-forces to not only survive but direct it.

As is apparent from listening to them, both perceive their world with a different eye—yet each generates an extraordinary degree of concern, warmth, fragility—and tenacity.

The recurring theme which threads through the book is the destiny of the people who find themselves in the eye of the racial storm that is America: a theme which is an undercurrent in their discussions, from *Superfly* to the possibilities of genocide.

This is an informal book—the tapings took place in Margaret Walker's home in November 1972 and at my Washington, D.C., apartment in January 1973—but it is by no means a casual one. The issues are approached with the idea of rendering not detailed theoretical analyses, but their empirical consequences.

Finally, it is an intense book and consequently there are many moments when the discussion becomes emotionally heated. I remember after one such exchange, which visibly drained both of them, Nikki had to leave for a prearranged appointment. I wondered if they were really angry at each other as Nikki silently put on her coat and started for the door. Suddenly she turned around, walked back toward Margaret who was still sitting on the sofa, and radiated one of those smiles that probably only two women who have felt so much and so deeply—about their men, their children, the meaning of their lives—can share in such a moment, and one which requires no explanation.

The Editor

Table of Contents

A Poetic Equation:

Two Views: One Destiny

Walker: (smiling) You know, Nikki, you and I belong to a mutual admiration society. I know a lot of people who think you are a brazen hussy. I happen to like you—hussy and all!

Giovanni: (laughs, then expression gets serious) I'll tell you this. I will tell you a difference between us. I grew up in a world that said the exception is the exception. You grew up in a world that said the exception is the rule.

Walker: The exception *proves* the rule is what I say.

Giovanni: O.K., let me explain what I mean. If *you* met two white people who were nice you'd say there were some of them worth saving. If *I* met two white people that were nice, I'd say, Hmm, too bad when we have to act against them to save ourselves. That's what I mean. To me an exception is an exception.

Walker: That *is* a very great difference between us. There may be something vacillatory about my position, and I hate vacillation. I don't like it at all. I like honesty. I like what *you* represent. I couldn't think of white people that way though, because I really genuinely believe in people everywhere. I know what the struggle of black people has been. I'm black, and I have been through some terrible stuff. Stuff that I cannot bear repeating because it is too painful, you understand? Three years ago, when they killed the students at Jackson

State College* it gave me diarrhea from which I have never recovered. Ever so often, as soon as I get upset or emotional, I get diarrhea like I did when I was pregnant and having babies. But it's a sickness that I've gotten from seeing what has happened to black people. A few weeks ago, they killed two more students at Southern.† This thing grieves me so deeply, it is down inside my flesh. The things that I see happening to black people across the country are just tearing me apart.

Before I die I want to make a certain statement about what our life is like here, but I want to add something that's not just about black people. I believe deeply in a common humanity. The black man belongs to the family of man. One part of that family is out of control—like a virus or cancer—and that is the white man. He and his technological society are bent on destroying the world. Everywhere the white man has gone with his empire, he has destroyed people, races, societies, cultures, and in the course of it, has sterilized himself. He is completely the mechanical man: without heart, without soul. He is the Tin Man of *The Wizard of Oz.*

But I *don't* believe that all the white people in the world are no good. There are some people of good will. I don't know what this country as a whole feels except what I see in the political elections, and I see the country going fascist. We have been going that route a long, long time. A lot of things the country has done from its inception were fascist. But now, now I think we are in the face of a terrible fascist dictatorship.

*Two students killed May 15, 1970, by Mississippi State and Jackson police on the campus. The Scranton Commission which reported on the incident stated that the firing by police into the dormitory windows without warning and without orders was "completely unwarranted and unjustified." Though the police alleged that they were reacting to sniper fire emanating from the upper dormitory windows, both students were killed at ground level with buckshot, though the use of birdshot had been the policy in former incidents of this kind.

†Two students killed November 16, 1972, by police on the Southern University campus, Baton Rouge, Louisiana. Governor Edwards acknowledged that a deputy sheriff might have mistakenly fired live ammunition into the group of students instead of tear-gas cannisters.

Now the difference between us is, well—I cannot exclude even the evil man from this business of common humanity.

G   Well, I'm pleased that I know you, because I think that's a *rare* position.

W *(responding quickly)* That's the way I've come up and I can't help but believe that. My children say to me, Mama, Mama, you still believe in Christianity, don't you? The white man's religion. See? I don't think I could be a Muslim. I don't think I could be a part of Islam. I respect Islamic culture and black people should know a lot about it. I think it ought to be taught in our schools. But I don't expect to ever join the sect. It may be because I'm old. Maybe because I'm middle-aged. Or is it because I believe in and I admire all religions deeply?

My father raised me to have respect for world cultures and world religions. My mother didn't feel that way. My mother and grandmother were fundamentalists. But my father was not. And that is why . . . (What I would like to say to you, I'm unable to say. I find myself almost inarticulate in trying and I shouldn't be because I've never been inarticulate.)

My father was a scholar. He was a scholar in terms of the ancient world. He knew so many things so well. He was really quite a man. He believed in books. He lived in a world of books. He was always hurt and disillusioned about the world outside, and about people, because he was always catching the hell of it, the persecutionism. Yet, I don't think he was ever paranoiac. My mother would have come closer to that than my father. I got my love for books and my desire to write from my father. He belonged to a family of people who for generations had been interested in culture, in languages and religions. Books and music, art—that is what I was formed to. I have high respect for him to this day because of it. My father may have been an intellectual snob. He *may* have been. My grandmother was always having to put his feet on the ground and tell him to speak to Miss So-and-

so who took in washing and ironing down the street, 'cause grandmama would remind him that she had taken in washing and ironing when her husband died, and she had to support her family. "You didn't speak to Miss So-and-so. She told me you passed right by there and you didn't speak. You can't do that to people. You get your living from the people." I grew up hearing that and watching my father being softened by it.

But my father was a man who spoke and read a number of languages. He knew Greek and Latin, French and Spanish and Hindustani. He'd speak Yiddish to the people in the marketplace. He said he had the blood of all races in his veins. He was a ginger-brown man who you knew was of African descent. You see? But he said there was Spanish, and there was German Jew, there was East Indian in his blood. It was the same thing that W.E.B. Du Bois used to say with pride about the different kinds of blood that flowed in his veins. I have always secretly felt that what mankind should be in an ideal sense is that mixture of people and races. I really believe in it. I don't think there is anything sacred in the integrity of race, white or black. You hear me? That's a strange feeling coming from me, but I believe in that. Anytime I degrade anybody some of that degradation subtracts from my spiritual self. I really believe that.

G We have a terrific difference of opinion because—

W I think that it cuts away at my humanity when I attack the humanity of anyone else.

G All right, but to allow yourself to be denigrated is some kind of idea that you are somehow better than the son-of-a-bitch that's doing it.

W I didn't say, I didn't say—

G I didn't say that you said it. I said what I think.

W Yes.

G I think that is one of the greatest differences between us. When they add up sides, it really doesn't matter. I didn't know your father. I don't care how he looked at himself. He counts on *our* side. Those other people go on the other side. What I care about is when the toll comes in.

W Do you want to split the world straight down the middle?

G I don't want to split the world, it's split already. And if that's the way it is, then I want my side to come out number one. That's what I know. Another difference between you and me is that I don't think of things as happening to black people anymore.

W You think we need to make things happen to other people.

G We must or we are encouraging people to act upon us.

W I will tell you I do believe that our common enemy is the white man in America and his culture which are striving to destroy us and our culture.

G Look, the minute I can tell you that you have run a game on me that game must stop, or I am running that game also!

W I want to ask you, Nikki, how do you suppose black people in this country at this particular point in time and history can take control—not only of their own destiny but of the destiny of America? That is what you are asking us to do.

G The two destinies are one and the same. And not only is it imperative but I think it is only natural that we do so.

W It can't be done by force, can it?

G Wait, don't answer your own question.

W I'm asking you.

G All right. I think we can look at it in terms of its simplest or most common denominator. If black people take over their own destiny then we have taken over the destiny of the world. The expression that you once used was that we are descendants of Africa, and I'm going to say something further—we are also the *inheritors* of America. We are the new race that you said in your poem, "to let the bloody peace be written, let a new race emerge." We are it.

Violence and the **11**
Decision to Respond

G One of the things I resented most growing up was that I heard all the time—I guess you heard it, too—that *I* had to be better. A little white kid that cannot read, and there're plenty of them, is still a little white kid. And, whatever he has to have, somebody will put an umbrella over him and see to it that he gets it. If he comes out of school illiterate, if he drops out of high school. . . .

W He'll get a job. He will still be hired.

G You know, we think it's something to be a telephone repairman. Anybody could do it, my three-year-old son, Tommy, could do it, because you put the yellow wire with the yellow wire, the blue with the blue. An illiterate could do that. But they will see to it that he becomes a linesman and after his ten thousandth line is laid, they kick him into the sales department. Then he talks to people who speak English as poorly as he does, and who don't give a damn because "John is a good old boy." And he does that for a while and then he becomes the vice president. A white kid is a white kid. Black kids don't have the right not to be better than anybody else.

W They should have the right to be bad as much as to be good.

G Yes, indeed, and my son is a perfect example of my philosophy. He has a right to scream on a train if he wants to.

7

W (*brusquely*) Let's stop right there! Let's stop right there and talk about that a minute. We differ on this question of permissiveness.

You raise your child to become a healthy, happy adult who can adjust to any situation and who can be an intelligent person, not only in a sterile society but in any society that he has to cope with. I am saying that I don't want to let my child feel like he has a right to yell fire in a crowded theater. He *hasn't* got a right to do it. He hasn't got the right either to just go along without any kind of control. A child has to be trained and in certain years, early years, at the age that Tommy is now, you need certain discipline. You have to have certain disciplinary controls so that the child will be able to move with a certain smoothness through the environment he has to live in, and that means certain controls—certain controls, not repression, and not suppression. He cannot exist in a libertarian fashion. Freedom means respect for certain natural, physical, moral, and spiritual laws. Your greatest freedom comes in being able to live within the limits of certain laws. And not to the point that you are chaining him, repressing him. Yes, discipline is part of life, too, Nikki.

G Yes, but you can overrespect—

W Yes, you can over and you can under. And striking the happy medium is what you've got to do.

G The hell with the happy medium. You've got to decide what you, yourself, want.

W Wait a minute, that's another thing. There's another difference in our generations and there again you may be a liberated soul and I may have thought in my generation that I was an emancipated person because I didn't think the way my mother thought. And you don't think the way your mother's generation thought, because I'm of her generation and I say the answer to life is not always in getting what I want. When you talk about what you want, you mean what you want for your child.

G Yes, and for myself.

W And for yourself. The answer is that happiness is not a thing that comes just by getting everything you want.

G I never said that, Margaret.

W What do you mean by knowing what you want?

G The first thing you have to be concerned with is your own functional existence. You cannot throw your life away, and if there's anything that I would want for my child, I would want him to value his life. That is what I am trying in my own little screwed-up way to do, to teach him to value his own feelings so that if he had to decide whether or not he was going to fight some dumb-ass war, he would say, "You've got to be kidding—"

W Would you stop a minute?

G Go on.

W I don't understand how you proceeded and arrived at the conclusions that you did from the premise you made. You know what you said? You said something about him thinking about his feelings and your thinking about your feelings so that he will know not to go to war. Those are not the same. How do you come to a conclusion like this? I want to ask you. You are saying *my* feelings, *his* feelings— what about other people's feelings?

G What about them?

W You don't give a damn? I do and I figure you've got to think about other people as much as yourself.

G   Don't . . . I mean, I resent the level of this conversation. I think it is unfair to say that because I would place my feelings . . .

W   Above everything else.

G   Wait, Margaret, can I finish my own sentence?

W   *(impatiently)* Yes, I'm waiting.

G   That I would place my feelings into perspective—

W   That's another thing.

G   You never gave me a chance because you kept screaming at me.

W   I'm sorry.

G   The first thing I think anybody has to do is to think about what they want as they face a situation. Now, my son . . .

W   *(opens her mouth as if to say something)*

G   Wait, wait, wait. My son may want to go to war and that will be his choice. What I don't want, and I'm just using that as an example, Margaret, which you well know, to say that he will have to make up his mind what he thinks is best for him. I would try to train him to always think of how he feels himself so that he will not blindly follow *even me*, which is one thing I am proud of about the three years Tommy has been on earth: he does not blindly obey me and I am pleased with that.

W   *(quickly)* Wait a minute, Nikki, wait a minute, hold it, just one second—stick a pin in it. It is one thing to develop a child to be self-reliant and an entirely different thing to teach him that selfishness is the highest law of life.

G I didn't say that!

W When you think only of yourself and you teach your child to respect only his feelings you are teaching him selfishness.

G I see nothing wrong with selfishness.

W Well, now, there are degrees of selfishness. I used to hear someone talk about the higher art of selfishness. There are certain times, yes, when you need to be selfish. But I contend that you cannot base a life—yours, your son's, or anyone else's—purely on one's personal wishes, wants, and desires.

G Well, if we're going to pursue this . . .

W And I think this is important. You see, this business of permissiveness—and we are facing this in the schools today —this is the problem that we have, and in an age of revolution this is a danger. A danger because we have been restricted so long, been repressed and oppressed and will not continue to be suppressed and we misunderstand the meaning of true freedom. We misunderstand the meaning of true personal freedom and we take it to such an extreme that the child coming into the classroom cannot be handled by another soul—only his mother, and sometimes not even his mother can do anything with him, and what happens is this: the mother comes and says I don't want you doing such and such to my child. I want my child to speak his own mind. I want my child to have the right to think the way he wants to think. I want my child to believe what he wants to believe. I want my child to be free and to act in any way he wants to act. Do you see where we're going there? Do you understand what is happening to us?

G   That is corrupt logic you're presenting to me.

W *(challengingly)* Corrupt logic? Well, you correct the logic that I have and show me what will happen to a child who is undisciplined, who believes that he has the right to do anything he feels like doing and his mother tells him the most important thing is to fulfill his personal wishes. You tell me what you mean by that. Qualify it or modify it and tell me where that leads.

G   O.K., I'm going to try. I'll stick with my example because maybe I can make sense out of it. I want my son to test things against himself. In order to be free, one must be able to take care of oneself as best one can. That doesn't say that everybody goes out and starts a little Mom and Pop Goodness Store. But one must function in this society with the people with whom one finds oneself. I want my son, Thomas, particularly my son, Thomas, and I think every child, to be able to function wherever he may be.

W When you say "function," what do you mean?

G   I mean—that's why I hate intellectual discussions. I mean that wherever he goes I want him to feel that he is still Thomas Giovanni. That he comes from someplace and is going someplace.

W That's important, that's very important.

G   That he is competent to judge and make decisions.

W That is right, all of that is right.

G   Now, in my opinion—to try to make it intellectual or something—in my opinion one of the things he needs is familiarity with skills and I would be in error as a mother if I did not insist that he acquire them.

W And learning to read is one.

G Wait, wait, wait, wait.

W But as soon as I join an issue, you see . . .

G I'm just trying to deal with things one at a time as you keep bringing them up.

W All right.

G In terms of discipline, he must know that in order to be free, he will have to be able to make decisions.

W That is not the logical conclusion. Freedom and decision, Nikki, those are not analogous.

G (change in tone and said aggressively) You know, niggers are not free because they could not decide what to do when the war was over!

W Is that the reason?

G That's three-fourths of it. They had no skills with which to accomplish anything.

W But, here again, we're dealing with the kind of reasoning that differs from generation to generation. And I am not criticizing yours anymore than I would accept criticism of mine.

G How many people, how many young men in Jackson are dead today because they couldn't make a decision about the damned war, because they had no skills, because they had no alternatives to saying, O.K., I'll join the Army?

W Which war are you talking about—Vietnam?

G   All of them, because it's stupid for a black man to have been in any of America's wars except the Civil War and they never completed what *that* began. After shooting on those Southerners they should have turned on those Northerners and then just fought it all out. But that's not what we have. What we have is a situation of black people, especially black men, particularly those who don't have the skills to make judgments, to make decisions about their own lives and their own life-styles. They are a dependent people.

W   Whom do you blame for this?

G   I'm not blaming anybody.

W   Where is the trouble, then?

G   The trouble is that they must learn . . .

W   Where? Learn where? Their mamas should teach 'em? You're saying their mothers didn't teach 'em.

G   Their mothers gave them what they had; their mothers didn't have much.

W   Well, I disagree with you. I disagree with you on several grounds. I go back to what I consider the strength in that black woman way back before the Civil War when she was just a slave. And I go back to the strength of what I think was in that black soldier who fought in the Civil War and what he tried to do after the war. I do not blame what happened to him on his basic inability to decide.

G   I do.

W   Then I think what you are saying is that the society, that the economy and the politics and the labor problems, the government, none of these things are determinants.

G Of course they are determinants, don't don't—

W But I'm saying this, those black people who lived a hundred and fifty or a hundred years ago faced odds they could not overcome. In the Reconstruction period, look at the men who went from these various Southern states into government halls—what did they face? When you talk about what they should have done, how many of them died doing just what you said they should have done? A lot of them died shooting it out; a lot of black people were killed in that period. Why? Because the Civil War was not over when Lee surrendered. The Southern whites turned on those blacks with everything, and that's why they intimidated them away from the polls with guns. Lynching was the law. And what was the decision the black man might have been able to make against that? How could he decide not to be lynched? How could he decide not to be killed?

In terms of labor, he actually tried to do a lot of things. He tried to go West; he was in the cowboy business, he was out there squatting on the land and homesteading just like everybody else. He struggled against the odds of poverty and ignorance just like everybody else. He wasn't just a weakling and a namby-pamby who couldn't make any decisions. That's wrong, and when you say it you have to go back and think about what you're saying because that was not entirely true. Our situation today is not wholly of our own making. And it hasn't been. Black people, you must remember, came in chains, the majority of us. Some did not come in chains, but they did very little for those who were in chains. And yet the Abolitionists were not all white. The Abolitionists were black too. There was an anti-slavery struggle that black people belonged to. Don't underestimate us and don't just sell us down the road and say we didn't do anything because we did.

G Now, Margaret . . .

W You know that. You know too that what happened in Africa wasn't all white or all black. It was a human situation. Blacks in tribal wars. Whites buying and selling and killing —all that was a part of it. History is not just one solid page of black and white. Teaching your child how to come up in the society is your prerogative. But don't blame the black man back in the Civil War years even for being indecisive. He had as much brains as the next fellow. He was a pawn in the social struggle and always remember that. I'm not trying to teach again; I sound like the teacher. I'm no Miss Teacher; but I sound like Miss Teacher.

But, I want to get back to this business of the child, because I think, Nikki, what happens to us as mothers is very important. Yes, it's extremely important. You have a wonderful child. You have a beautiful baby and you want to do everything you can for that child so that when he grows up he can face the world and he can be a man, and he can make decisions. But you want to be careful in your own logic that you do not confuse your affection and your love and your devotion for this child and your desire to do what is right for him in such a way that he becomes an anti-social, anti-people person.

How do I bring him up so that he remains lovable and desirable? How do I raise him so that he can insulate himself? That's what you want, you want him insulated against the hurts that even *you* have experienced. You want him able to stand on his own feet, and the last thing in the world that's important is being able to make a living, because you figure his instincts are going to help him find out a way to make money. That's not the important thing. You want the personality of your child developed the best way you possibly can.

We as black people today, and especially in this generation, are in an age that threatens to be an age of anarchy. Because we have undergone such tyranny the danger is great of our going to an extreme—an extreme of anarchy in order to resolve and dissolve the tyranny. And when you talk about decision-making—control is what I'm talking

G   But the thing that I'm saying is that today, and this is what I'm trying to impress upon you—at least give me the respect for my viewpoint. . . .

W   I want to, I want to . . .

G   Without being nasty about it.

W   *(good-heartedly)* Well, now wait a minute, wait a minute. I am wholly in respect of your viewpoint, and if I am nasty that's my disposition.

G   I know you, Margaret, I'm not going to let you do that to me. What I'm trying to say is that today we must draw upon all the strengths.

W   That's the word—the strengths, not the weaknesses.

G   I didn't say it was a weakness. I said that there was an inability to make decisions.

W   That was weak, wasn't it?

G   No, if you don't have the skills to make a decision, if you don't feel you are enough of a person to make a decision, you will not make decisions. For example, I can't believe that Mark Essex climbed up on top of that Howard Johnson's Motel because he hated.* I cannot believe that, and his mother won't say that. She said, "My son was tired."

W   Of all the trouble.

G   His mother said, "My son will be a man." If *my* son, whom I love dearly and would hate the thought of having

*In January of 1973 Mark Essex climbed upon a rooftop of a Howard Johnson Motel in New Orleans, Louisiana, and fired his gun at people below. There were seven killed and twenty-one wounded. However there is speculation as to the number shot by Essex, and the number shot by the police in their pursuance of him.

G *(voice rises)* Can I tell you what I think they should have done?

W *(quietly)* Yes.

G When they passed a law that said that black men must turn in their weapons, they should have fought.

W They shouldn't have turned them in?

G No, they shouldn't have.

W *(sarcastically)* They could have killed 'em off like that.

G You asked what I thought should happen. Did I answer it? Now I didn't rhetorize behind what you said with satirical remarks.

W Now, how am I making satirical remarks? I apologize.

G That did not happen and I do not have any less respect for the decisions made. The decisions made now must be used to...

W That's happened. Now, we're in another day.

G In another day. The young men coming back from Vietnam, which is a war that I have deplored, are not turning in their weapons!

W They're not going to have the same attitude they did after World War I, the Civil War. . . .

G Not even Korea. The men come back here . . . somebody is shooting cops all over this country, which I'm sure you've read about.

W I've been watching it, looking at it.

about, how much control, because you see we've had too much control and you are afraid of that. You don't want too much control, but I say there's got to be some.

G Do I get a chance? I resent the whole emotional level of this discussion.

W Emotional level! Well, now, do you want to put it on another level? You say you can't stand intellectual stuff. You don't want to get into something intellectual. Now you are resentful of the emotional thing. Just which level do you want to put this on?

G *(sighs and smiles)* I'm a woman, I can change my mind.

W You're a woman is right. So am I and—

G And I think it's unfair for you to sit here . . .

W And lecture you in this fashion.

G No, I don't mind your lecturing me, you've earned that right. But I think it's unfair to say that I have no respect for the Civil War story; that's not what I'm saying.

W *(in a quieter and almost motherly tone)* Well, I didn't say that, honey. I think you have a lot of respect, but you did say this: The trouble was that they didn't know what to do.

G I said that part of it was that they did not.

W What do you think they should have done?

G No, see, I cannot . . . I mean I can tell you what I think they should have done because—

W But then you were—

any bullet in him, let alone a hundred, decided to climb atop a building, I want to have that much strength to know that I reared him to be a man. That was Mark's decision. His mother did not tell him, "Son, go climb up there and shoot some folk." He made a decision and she backed him afterwards and that's the kind of woman I hope I am. With any man in my life.

W Wait a minute. There's some confusion here.

G There's no confusion to me.

W No, there's some confusion. In my mind I'm confused, if you're not. I feel this way. Again, there is a great difference, a gulf, between our ages and minds; between the thirties and the sixties. I said five years ago, the very week that Martin Luther King, Jr., was killed, that Vietnam is an immoral war and I'd rather see my son go to jail than fight in that war.

G But you couldn't make that decision for Siggy.*

W I didn't. To my consternation, he volunteered for the marines and I thank God he got home. This is the thing that I felt: While my son was away, I was sick unto death. A tick was in my face. I just looked something frightful and I was so nervous I couldn't sleep more than four hours a night. I made napkins, I made flowers, I embroidered, I couldn't sleep at night. I would wake up hearing him say, "This time I'm dead, Mama, I know I'm dead." I'd see him down in marshy places—he was actually in those places. He was actually saying that. He told me that one time he saw a man point a gun at him and he ducked and felt the heat as the bullet went by. That close. Another time three buddies were sitting down on the ground and he looks at this buddy and he looks at that buddy, and when he looks at the third buddy he sees him blown to pieces ten feet in front of him. I haven't begun to tell it—the horror, the horrendous

*Margaret Walker's son, Siggy Alexander.

experience. And now I realize—and it's not just my weakness—I had this great fear that if my son got into a battle he would be killed. My son got into plenty of battles and he didn't get killed. That's wonderful.

But I'd love to stop and analyze something you said and see if I understand it correctly. I said this is the difference, the great distinction between us. You know how I feel about that boy Essex? I don't feel that he was a great hero at all. Getting up there and killing all of those people and being riddled. He might have been in *your* estimation a man.

G Yes.

W I also feel that the boy was in great turmoil and emotionally sick of the stuff he had seen. And I think this: I'm not so sure that that is a sign of strength. I am not so sure. Now, I don't believe everything I read in the papers about how filthy his room was and all the dirty words and all the hate that he had written on the walls there. But I do know that every black man who comes back from Vietnam is inoculated with a virus of hate for the white man in this country. I know he has it. I don't know that that's necessarily great spiritual strength, to have deep hatred and feel that the only thing he can do is kill some of these "honkies." I am not so sure that it is, I am not so sure.

G I respect Essex.

W I think that any time a person is so completely, completely disjointed from the world in which he lives that he feels the only way out for him is to shoot and kill, there is not only something wrong with the society but there has to be something wrong with him, too.

G May I say something about Nikki Giovanni?

W Yes.

G   O.K. I have a habit; I'm twenty-nine years old now so
it's pretty much ingrained in me. I generally look at things
as a choice, as it's either-or, you know? That I am pro-
abortion because for one thing I hate child abuse.

W   That's . . .

G   Wait—I'm just trying to say something about my own
logical faculties.

W   I'm not following you.

G   You're not following me, O.K. I look at things in terms
of what would happen "if," and I look for the widest possible freedom for the individual to make a decision. Essex,
I think, had limited choices to begin with. From what I can
understand about the young man, he seemed to be very
sensitive, he seemed to have come from a wonderful family.
He dropped out of college and enlisted in the navy. He
was less than honorably discharged. He came out and identified what bothered him. What he *could* have done is beat
his wife, if he had one.

W   Which would have been much more immoral and
cruel and ugly.

G   Because he wasn't mad at his wife. He could have had
a bunch of kids, that he . . .

W   Couldn't feed.

G   Not only couldn't feed, but hated. He could have become a fearful young man in his community. He could have
been one of those guys that every Friday night has to go
down and kill a nigger.

W   Are they the only choices he had, Nikki?

G   No, I'm not saying that, Margaret. I'm just saying what I looked at was a young man that could have been all those things we've seen so many times before with *us* absorbing his anger. Essex made a decision. He made a decision and he carried it through and on that level, which is why I'm saying that I have ultimate respect for him. Black people today, young black people—my generation if you want to call it— are saying that if you want to play Nazi, we will not play Jew. And I think that the events that we're seeing are possibly going to make the whole community much more repressed. For we have put the world on notice that we are not going to be lined up and I think that that is very significant because I don't think America gives a damn about lining us up. They would like to. We have said, you can try, but we are fighting back. And our young men are in the forefront of this battle.

W I don't believe individual defiant acts like these will make for the revolution you want.

G No, don't ever misunderstand me and my use of the term "revolution." I could never believe that having an organization was going to cause a revolution. America is known for absorbing and infiltrating. One thing the papers keep saying about this so-called Black Liberation Army is that the Establishment can't infiltrate it, and, you know, they can't infiltrate it because it does not exist. There is really no such thing as a Black Liberation Army. There are people they have trained to be their killers who are now back to kill them.

W I admire your generation. I know that I could not at all be the same as your generation. I wouldn't want to be. I lived and came of age in a time that I thought was exciting. It certainly wasn't as highly tensioned as the time we're living in now.

But, I think both of us have this concern, what is going to happen to our people in this country? I don't know that any of us can come up with a solution, just as we are never able completely to state all the ramifications of the problem. But, it seems to me that if we could formulate our different ideologies to come up with our different points of view and just stand them up there and stack 'em up where we could look at them, that we would discover that the whole racial picture has not only changed amazingly in the last thirty years but that our technological society has given it a completely different twist. My feeling for Essex is one of great sympathy and, I would hope, for understanding, but I also feel a great deal of pity for what society had done to that young man. I don't feel his life is wasted. I just have never believed that solutions come in isolated, individual packages. Roles may. The role-playing may be individual, but the solutions are not. Maybe he's part of the solution. Maybe the answer is in the violent outbursts and maybe in this racial confrontation and conflict. Well, now, how otherwise would you respect his action? You figure, well at least he made a decision, he was able to stand up to the decision, he carried it out and you respect him for that.

G   If that young man had died in Vietnam, with the waste, with the same hundred bullets in him for having shot seven Vietnamese . . .

W   Nobody would think anything about it.

G   We would not be discussing it. He would still be dead. He made a statement. He made a decision and he made a statement. Let me put it another way. Someone once said that history was the biography of great men. I don't believe that. And, on the other hand, history is not just a chronicle of events, either.

W   It's people.

G   People are a part of it.

W Michael Harper says history is your own heartbeat, whereas Jay Wright says it's death.* Death is history.

G I can't believe that. What I have seen and the way I read history—and we all read history to suit ourselves—is that certain individuals have taken certain tasks upon themselves. In some cases, they were successful, in some cases, unsuccessful in their own terms, but they have helped to shape the way people think.

For example, we were speaking of Thurgood Marshall before we started taping. Who would have thought when that young man was a lawyer coming out of Howard, taking school desegregation cases, that he would one day sit on the Supreme Court; that he would have won his case and received the accolade he did? And just as Thurgood has a place in history, so does Essex. Because Thurgood made a decision to fight that way, you understand what I'm saying?

W I understand you.

G And Essex made a decision to fight his way.

W I understand that.

G And to me we can not take away either. And there are people, as you well know, who would take away what Thurgood did. There are people who would take away what Martin Luther King did. There are people who would take away what Malcolm X did. And I think that we, as people who try to give voice or meaning to some of these actions, must know that we must put them all together to make a history of the people. And what I fear today, what I deeply fear today, is that if we do not have what you call these isolated incidents, we as a people would be in even more serious trouble. It is not the trouble of lynching the nigger today

*Two black poets.

that we went through in the 1890s up to World War I. It is not the urban decay that we went through after that war and going into World War II. It is not just the Depression, it is not just sending some black people over to Korea or something. We're talking about the possibility of annihilating a people. It's alway been on that level, you know. Some people have always felt that there was a good chance that we would be annihilated.

W I never have believed it's going to come off.

G I don't believe it and I think that history will bear that out, that you cannot wipe out a people. A blood line is a very strong thing. But I believe that it is difficult for anyone, any group, to exist with ten or twelve million of its members stacked up. One of the reasons I think war in the Middle East continues is that the Jews are trying to show the world that they have balls. Had they stood up in Germany against the Germans, who were killing them, the way they now stand up against the Arabs, with whom they possibly—as far as I read—could have made peace, the world would be different.

What we know is that American blacks have no place to go. We speak of Africa, we speak of getting out. Some of us will, most of us will not. Most of us will live and die here and I say that I have ultimate respect for people who are making decisions and saying you are on notice, we will fight back. Because a war has been going on. The Panthers were wiped out. Those were nice young men, by any standard. They were not hurting anybody. Mark Clark and Fred Hampton were in bed when the police came in to shoot them.* You understand what I mean? They were just young men trying to respond to a problem. They can infiltrate the Panthers and they did, because they were organized, they put on their berets and their jackets, they said

*Black Panthers killed by police in Chicago on December 4, 1969.

we are Panthers and this is our program. They cannot do anything with those Vietnam veterans except pray for them.

W I said the other day I really don't believe that the government is going to bring 'em back in here en masse. I don't believe they'd dare.

G Well, they claim that there's only six hundred POW's. They can bring back 600 men if they can get them on dope, which is what they've been trying to do—Vietnam is the second Opium War. You know, I would not want Essex to have been my son, but if he had been, I would pray that I carried myself as well as his mother has.

W Well, I think the woman acted with dignity.

G And I think that she shows an understanding of her son and the times in which he lived. And all she could say was if this would help someone to understand the terrible burdens that we all must carry, that perhaps it would not have been in vain.

W That's all very well, but I am not willing for the benefit of the young black who's coming along and who faces this terrible kind of death every day, I'm not willing to set up a heroic example of violence in any form.

G But see—that is a real disagreement. That is a real disagreement.

W Between us, yes.

G (intensely) Yes, indeed, because we have been subject to some of the most horrendous violence. We find that love is not the opposite of violence. Love does not stop violence. Nonviolence is not the antithesis of violence. It does not stop violence.

W And love is not the opposite of hate?

G No.

W What, then, would you say is the antithesis of non-violence and what's the antithesis of love?

G The antithesis of love is indifference.

W Well, then, you and I don't agree on anything.

G And I think that the answer to violence is a response.

W A violent response to violence?

G One must respond.

W But, baby, you're not going to tell me that violence is the opposite of violence, are you?

G No, I'm not.

W Our reasoning processes just don't go the same way.

G That's a word game. Don't misunderstand what I mean. Because that's a word game that *we're* playing. *(voice sharpens)* I know that if you stand in here beating the living shit out of me that the only way that I can stop you is to beat you back. Frederick Douglass said it much more eloquently —even if I lose, I have hurt you. Even if I lose, you will think twice.

That boy Frazier, poor Frazier, stood there and won that fight from Ali and Ali beat him down and put him in the hospital for two months and by the time he got to Foreman, he had to think twice before Foreman floored him. You fight and you fight. Maybe if someone were to come in this door right now and my son would be there, you understand, and I would be protecting him maybe I would get hurt.

Maybe I wouldn't be able to protect him completely, but I would do enough damage so that the next time when he had to go up against them they're a little bit weaker. And that's the whole situation of blacks against whites, because if I am reading the situation right, now we are admitting maybe we cannot win. But goddamn, if you are going to drag us like bleeding sheep we are not going to go out loving you. It won't happen, those days are *over*! They have had our love and they didn't know what to do with it.

W I think people misunderstand this whole business of what my generation felt and feels about hatred and violence and love and nonviolence. My integrity is violated by my own hate, by my own bitterness, and by my own violence. It isn't what I do to the other fellow that hurts me so much as what I do to myself when I do something to the other fellow.

G Well, *I* can take that burden. I can take that weight.

W Well, I don't want it.

G I'll take it for you!

W I'm not going to teach my child that the only way you can answer tyranny is with hatred and violence.

G Margaret, I didn't say that. You've read Frantz Fanon?

W Yes.

G O.K., Dr. Fanon says it is only logical, if I may paraphrase him, that if someone is abusing you it is healthy to stop that abuse. Should you refuse to stop that abuse, it will sicken you.

W That's right. I agree with that and I know what you are saying. But I'm saying this, that there's a certain amount of aggression involved in the whole business. And I think it'll take a whole generation after you, a generation after your child to wipe out not just the blood and the violence and the hatred, but what the thing will do to *us*.

G   I'm not going to disagree, but I'm going to say that if I were attacked, I would defend myself, and if you were going to sit here and say, "Well, Nikki, you were violent," I'm going to say, right!

W   No, that's not what I'm saying.

G   I said the responses to the police and you said that's violence and I said if that's violence, fine. I'm not going to debate what to call it.

W   We started out with Essex and you said that he made the decision to go up there and kill those people.

G   He did, he did. And I consider that a response. And I think there will be more responses. That the violence hurled against us will be met and if you want to say with violence, I am going to say, yes, I can take the weight because I cannot take the weight of a constant degradation. I cannot, it is too much. I do not value seeing my contemporaries, the men that I've known . . . I don't like to see their riddled bodies. And I don't like the fact even that they're in jail, I don't like the way that they are being attacked and I am pleased that they respond. I am proud that they respond. And they must respond because otherwise they would be unhealthy. Black people, whether any of us like it, have given up on trying to reform white people.

W   Well, I don't think we can do that.

G   Nobody thinks so. And they're saying you must get off my back. There's a play in Manhattan right now called *The River Niger* and one of the characters is an airman. He said that somebody had grabbed almost every piece of him. When he finally got to the air force, all that he owned was his big toe. And when they started grabbing that, he said get off my toe. And that's the way people feel. We have tried. We cannot overlook how we have tried. We have tried to say we are harmless; we have tried to say we bear no ill toward you; we have tried to say that despite you we will love you. When they shot King, that was *their* shooting. We didn't shoot King. They couldn't find a black man to kill him because if they could, you know they would have. But they couldn't even import a nigger to kill him. That was not true of Malcolm. We pulled that trigger, if we want to really look at Malcolm X's death. Black men could pull the trigger, black men did pull the trigger. They could hire themselves some killers to kill Malcolm for whatever reason. But with King, I don't care what SCLC says, I don't care what Lyndon Johnson said, I don't care what any of them say, they killed a dream.

W They killed the dreamer.

G No, they killed the *dream*! Nobody wants to save those people anymore and that is what you are seeing. We *want* to say you can kill the dreamer but not the dream, but the dream is dead! Because it was personified in Martin and when they killed Martin, they told everybody, love me if you want to but I'll shoot you too. So somebody said hey, I'm not going to waste my time. I will deposit my love where it can be useful. And I will respond if you get on my toe. And I am pleased that it is just the way it is. That there is no such thing as any of this shit they're trying to make it. There's no such thing as any Liberation Army. There is none. That's just something that they would like to create so they can send their undercover agents in.

W An excuse to shoot somebody.

G And the people they get will not be the people who are doing it. They got poor Ahmed Evans up there in Cleveland. One reason that boy is still alive is they know he did not shoot those people. He did not shoot those cops. Those two white cops that were killed in Cleveland? They don't know who did it. They will pick up whom they can and try to harass people, but the people who are doing it are very serious.

W But, Nikki, where do you think all the killings and the hatred is going to go and how much of it has got to come off before it's all over?

G I will not accept a combination of killing and hatred. I say again, I don't think that Essex was hate-ridden. Because I think if he had been hate-ridden, he would have gone in there and shot his mama and daddy.

W He sure as hell wasn't love-ridden.

G I think that we have to look at the positives of his response, which was at least a healthy one. Emotional words like love and hate when you talk about murder are kind of foolish. Out of something like 650 murders that were committed in the city of Detroit according to the 1971-1972 statistics, 590 were committed by black people against black people. Now *that* was love. *That* was love. That was you go to bed with my woman, or you're my best friend and we start arguing 'cause we're drinking and I knifed you, I shot you. That was love. I don't think that love and hate are words to use when you talk about an Essex. I think the man was tired.

And, as Stokely said, *if* you are going to be a killer then you must decide whom you are going to kill. And Stokely was talking about the war. He said if you are going to be a killer, you must decide. Usually soldiers don't have love *or* hate. There is an enemy who must be destroyed and you fight a losing battle. And I said again, I will put Essex up there with all the rest of them who have fought battles. With *all* the rest of them: With Malcolm and with King and everyone else. And we can say, well, he's not glamorous, or he never left a decent note or did you see the shit on his walls and all that, but the fact is the man made a decision and acted it through. He identified what bothered him and decided he would do the best he could. And I agree that in Louisiana we have as yet to be told the full truth. All I'm saying is that people are responding to these actions. And the police are scared.

W You think they are?

G Oh, definitely. There's no disputing that. They are scared. And the problem is that they are going to get sub-machine guns to respond and they are going to shoot a bunch of innocent people which is going to, what the rev-olutionaries would say, "politicize" those families. They shot a boy called Rabbit in New Jersey. Did you read about that case? Now you know that's a shame because that boy wasn't doing anything but returning a traffic sign with his white friends. That's all he was doing. The boy wasn't doing anything. They shot a boy in D.C. over a stolen bike. Over a stolen bike, Margaret!

W But this has always happened.

G But it's *unacceptable*. And that's what people are say-ing. It is unacceptable. I wrote a poem once that said, "what 'always is' is not the answer. What never will be, must come."

W I think that when all the fighting and killing are done there's got to be some kind of reconciliation on some kind of basis other than a gun. I think there's got to be some kind of understanding.

G I am existential enough to say we cannot have recon-ciliation until *all* the killing is done.

W That's why we're very different.

G How can you reconcile—who's going to walk up to Patrick Murphy of the New York Police Department and say, "Well, listen, Pat, let's make peace?" Who can do it?

W Well, I think this, Nikki. As I look at the police war against black people that's been going on now. . . .

G Since the sixties.

W Yes, we saw the police in the sixties, but it was not until Daley said shoot to kill that we began to have the overt police shoot-outs. That is shooting on the basis that these people are not just "restless natives" but—

G Enemies. That they were black enemies.

W The "violent" blacks. That's what they called them— violent blacks.

G I said since the sixties because I identify the beginning of the police action . . .

W With King's demonstrations in Birmingham?

G Yes.

W That's when they put the police dogs on them.

G That's when they put the police dogs on the people, the fire hoses. I saw them ride the horses through the people in Mississippi. I saw them take the big horses out in San Francisco through the women and children. To trample women and children—white women and children. You know, when you talk about Daley's thing you have to keep in mind that was in 1968 and that was over white kids; they shot white kids at Kent State and anybody that's black knows that if they would shoot four white kids at Kent State and kill 'em, what they would do to us.

W Now they've shot four black students at Southern and Jackson, but they had also shot 'em at Orangeburg and Houston before any of that.

G All I'm saying is that we have recognized that we are at war. I may be so liberal as to say it's not even as racial as some of us think it is.

W Wait a minute. Let me say this, Nikki, and it just comes to me that this is something I may be wrong about, but it is my feeling that this business of getting up on the rooftop and shooting and killing, this business of making the violent response, answer the police, shoot any way you can is like starting at the worm's end and cutting it off. You know how the worm can be put back together, you know how you cut the snake, but until you amputate that snake's head— you understand? Cutting the snake in half won't kill it. Now, police are lackeys. They are underlings. They are the tools of the government and until you do something to the head of the system of control, you haven't gotten anywhere. The people who are in control are not in the street for you to shoot. And they don't deal with the guns. The response has got to be very different from an individual shooting two or three people or killing five to ten.

G I think that's part of the corruption of the so-called black thinkers, the Negro thinkers.

W What?

G That we constantly intellectualize what is happening. You were talking about policemen, who can be compared to soldiers—they're both lackeys of the government. Now, I don't know how many generals the Vietnamese killed, but I know they killed some forty-six thousand men, probably more than that. I know at one point I read at least fifty thousand.

W Probably didn't kill any generals.

G They probably didn't, but they won the war because for every line of soldiers that were sent to them, they cut them down. They said send some more, we're going to cut them down. It's taken them twenty years, something like that. This war started right after Korea and it's just now ending.

W Oh, no. That war those Vietnamese had been fighting a thousand years.

G I mean we got into it right after Korea. But they have been fighting back. They didn't say it's pointless to kill the soldier, let us wait until the President comes. They didn't say it is pointless to kill the private first-class, let us wait until we can find a general. They said if you send him, and he comes, we will try to kill him. If we do not kill him, we will injure him, and if we do not injure him and he gets us, he will still know that he was in a battle. America lost its first war because of that attitude.

W I agree.

G And I'm saying that, as far as I can see, that's what black people are saying. Which is with neither my advocacy nor my blessings, because they don't need either. Can you understand what I'm saying?

W Understand? I'll try with my "feeble" mentality. *(laughs)*

G *(smilingly)* Black women are so vicious.

If we can begin to understand and act upon the right as well as the necessity for people to think for themselves, to weigh—

W Oh, honey, that's the whole bag. Once we do that we have arrived at the millennium.

G *(frustratedly)* But, Margaret, you can see why that doesn't happen because of the discussion that we've been having! When I said I want my son to think for himself—

W That's all right, that's self-reliance. But you also—

G I want him to decide what he wants—

W That's good. That's fine.

G But then you carry it to his being undisciplined.

W But self-reliance is a different thing from permissiveness and lack of discipline or control.

G I never said that it wasn't, Margaret.

W This is what you did say. When you were talking about individual rights, personality and the entity of the individual, and teaching the child to value them, I go along with that. What you remarked, though, was that it depends on what you want, and what you want for him, and you said that all that mattered were his wishes—

G You're slanting my words.

W No, I didn't slant them a bit. I took exactly what you said and—

G I'm not going to back off of you even if it sounds, you know . . .

W No, no.

G Because what I'm saying is that people must think for themselves.

W That's right.

G   In the context of thinking for themselves, they must decide what they want.

W   That's all right. All that is O.K.

G   I don't like Cartesian logic at all, because I do not believe that one can start with, "I think, therefore I am." I don't think that works. I think that it has to be given.

W   "I am, therefore I think."

G   No.

W   You don't believe that?

G   Just "I am." You don't even begin to question that you are. We cannot begin to question whether or not we live in a world with people that we have to function with. That's silly. I mean I can't even find a better word for it. It's silly. Of course we live in a world, of course we interact. That's given. The question is, how in our interaction with each other do we get the things that sustain us? And how do we give what we need to give without giving away the essence of ourselves?

W   That's an entirely different thing from what you said before.

G   That's what I was trying to say, but you were screaming at me.

W   Oh. What you were trying to say and what you were saying were two different things; and you have said two different things here. You did not say the same thing in the beginning. That's a perfectly different point of view that you have expressed just now.

G   Well, that's what I meant. That's what I was trying to say.

W   Well, that's more positive.

G   But that's the same thing.

W   It is not the same thing, Nikki, and you are not going to put that over on me.

G   I'm not trying to put anything over on you.

W   You see, it is not the same. You said a different thing.

G   I'll have to read the transcript.

W   Yes. Do that.

G   *(to the editor)* Did I say a different thing?

W   She's not going to be a judge in this. She's not our referee.

G   You mean we're in this fight with no referee? No one is going to ring a bell?

(both laugh)

Chapter **III**

Content and Intent: Some Thoughts on Writing, Criticism and Film

W Nikki, let's talk a little about literature.

G O.K.

W You know, when I teach black literature I go back to what it was like in the early nineteenth century and then the post-Civil War period, and the early twentieth century, talking about Du Bois, Chesnutt, Dunbar. Of course, later comes James Weldon Johnson as a forerunner of the Harlem Renaissance, and bridges the period between Du Bois and the twenties, and at the same time a part of the twenties. He gave us that black preacher in *God's Trombones.*

Each of these decades, each of these periods is linked one to the other. Black literature is connected like a chain, with people who are influential in one period knowing and influencing folk in the next. The men who were the giants in the Harlem Renaissance had an influence on the thirties and the forties; for example, a man like Richard Wright, who began this series of major writers that included himself, Baldwin, Ellison, and Killens and coming up with people like Chester Himes and William Gardner Smith.

Gwendolyn Brooks dominated the decade of the fifties with poetry even though she didn't actually publish much then. She wrote *A Street in Bronzeville* and published it in 1945. *Annie Allen* was published in 1949 and got the Pulitzer Prize in 1950 and the whole decade of the fifties is

41

dominated by her. I think she says that her next major works came really at the end of the fifties and the beginning of the sixties, despite the fact that she was the key literary figure referred to during the fifties, except for people like Baldwin and Ellison—and Wright, of course, was still alive, but was out of the country during all of the fifties.

G I would say James Baldwin was the key literary figure.

W Of the fifties? You think so?

G And LeRoi Jones has been the figure . . .

W Of the sixties. And for a while I thought we might have expected Don Lee for the seventies, but I don't know now. I'm a little concerned as to who the key figure is. But the influence of Baraka on the whole decade was a kind of seminal source, the seed of the renaissance, the Black Renaissance of the sixties in literature.

G I prefer what you had to say about chains in literature. When I look at the sixties and then I look back at the fifties, I see no renaissance at all.

W But a gradual development and progression?

G Yes, the Harlem Renaissance is the most identifiable period as a renaissance because it was bursting. But I have not seen the flames die to be rekindled. And I think the terms we are using when we say the Black Renaissance or the explosion of the poets or whatever in the sixties are *commercial* terms and not scholastic or intellectual terms. Everybody calls it the New Black Poetry, but I think that the influence of Langston Hughes . . .

W Was very great. He was the first person after Dunbar to introduce a true black idiom into poetry in terms of the language. My mother said the other night she had a feeling that Ernest Gaines's language was somewhat like that. She thought of Gaines's language when she thought of Jesse B. Semple.

G   What was she reading, *The Autobiography of Miss Jane Pittman?*

W   No, the short stories—"Just Like A Tree." And I said, yes, but Langston was always urban, he was never rural. And there is a great difference between Langston's language and Ernest Gaines's. Ernest Gaines is always rural. He's dealing with the Louisiana folk culture, Creole and Cajun, whereas Langston met Jesse B. Semple in a bar, in a tavern, possibly up in Harlem.

G   Small's?

W   Beyond that, beyond Small's place. Up around a hundred and fifty-fifth street, at the edge of Washington Heights: on the hill, on Sugar Hill. I remember going with him one night when a place was just opening. It had the kind of amosphere out of which Semple came.

G   The fact that he read in bars influenced the attitudes, you know, the relationship between the poet and the audience.

W   Yes, which affected the language he used. Then come on to your own language and what the Establishment black and white was horrified to hear—the four-letter words. And especially, as I said in Chicago, a poem that Margaret Danner mentioned in the workshop, "The Essence of Mother Fucker." This belongs strictly to the sixties.

G   Do you realize that Kipling wrote a poem that had a line in it, which I love, that said that there are nine and sixty ways of perfecting tribal lays. *(laughs)*

W *(not laughing, with a puzzled expression on her face)* Of perfecting tribal lays?

G   You don't understand?

W   I'm afraid I didn't catch it. Is it a sexual connotation?

G   The sixty-nine is a *strong* sexual connotation. And that was Kipling.

W   That reminds me of the traumatic experience of Richard Wright literally trying to throw me out of the whole city of New York (I don't know what gave him the feeling that he had such authority). He and some others sent a card to Chicago. They sent one to Bob Davis* and one to me and it was signed the Sixty-Six Trio, and when Bob saw it he said, "Oh, my God, the dirty rascals, why would they do this to you, why would they do such a thing." I said, "What?" It went completely over my head.

G   The Sixty-Six?

W   The Sixty-Six Trio. Signed by the Sixty-Six Trio. And it carried a strong sexual connotation. He said, "Those niggers must have been drunk." But afterwards I told Langston just what I thought about him and all of 'em for it. I think we were up at Yaddo† and I told him I thought it was such a dirty thing and they sent it through the mail: "Of course, Margaret Walker is a talker. When she came to town what she said put Ted in bed and turned Dick upside down." *(both laugh)*

G   Who is Ted?

W   Theodore Ward.‡

---

*An actor and friend of Margaret Walker's.
†A retreat for artists established for them in 1922.
‡A prominent playwright in the thirties.

G Oh, that's who you were going with?

W Who? Not me. I never went with Ted Ward. He never was my boyfriend. People tried to make this kind of thing between Wright and me and I keep denying it over and over. I have protested it to the point that I realize now it's better to stop because I've protested so much that people think I've over-protested and they still give it the same connotation. I insist that we were not sweethearts, not ever. I didn't understand what his possible interest in me was.

But to get back to this business of language. In the twenties and thirties, for the first time we had the use of black speech from the streets. We were responsible for that particular urban idiom going into the American language.

G It was the first time because we were becoming urban. I think one of the things we forget when we start our critiques is that we could not have had a street language earlier. Speech had been plantation and southern and rural. And as we moved to the cities during the migration period, we developed a street language.

W I think that's an important point. Did you know Langston?

G No.

W Well, you really missed something.

G Yeah. But I remember Melvin Tolson. I met Melvin and he was the first person who tried to explain LeRoi Jones. *(smile)*

W Yes. . . .

G Who made sense out of what LeRoi Jones wrote, because I had not, of course, seen any of his plays. I was at Fisk University where you didn't see any of LeRoi Jones's plays.

I remember Melvin saying, "Why, that young man is telling us the country is a toilet." And it made sense because I considered the country a toilet.

W It *is* a toilet.

G And I said I must find that book. But I also lived in Cincinnati, Ohio, right? So the combination of Nashville, Tennessee, which has "no" book stores, and Cincinnati, Ohio, which had "no" book stores, made it very difficult until I found some people from Detroit. Vaughn started his bookstore, Ellis started his, John Killens had told me about Miss Jones—and then you begin to write these places and say, do you have? That's how I met Curt Ellis. I ordered some books and he didn't send them to me. I wrote him back and called him a Negro, and he was the first one to tell me he was not a Negro, and I have that letter—I have his and he has mine. He wrote me back and he said, "Dear Miss Giovanni, I am not a Negro. I consider myself a *black man* and you are right, I did not take care of business." I had ordered these books a long time and paid him for them right away, since I'm not good at paying my bills. So he sent me my money back and sent me two Chester Himes books. He still didn't send me the books that I ordered, but that's how I first began to know Curt Ellis.

But to go back to the evolvement of our literature—I think we make a mistake when we take a commercial term as a literary term.

W Well, when I speak about an explosion and the renaissance in the sixties, perhaps a better term would be the "mushrooming" of young black poets all over the country. For the first time it wasn't just New York. New York has always been a mecca for artists and writers and musicians and actors, people of the theater, dancers, and so on. They always felt you had to go to New York for success, because the big publishing houses were there, the big critics were there. Everybody gravitated toward New York.

G   What about Chicago?

W   Chicago is a different city and Chicago is very important in American literature for whole generations of writers,
both white and black. I mention the whites first not because
I mean to put them out in front, but when I think about
Hemingway and Sherwood Anderson and even Dreiser and
Carl Sandburg, I think about Chicago. Richard Wright spent
ten years there that were very important in his life. He developed as a writer there. He got his Marxist-Leninist education in Chicago. Langston, I think about seeing for the first
time in four years in Chicago in 1936, at the National Negro
Congress, and that was when he introduced me to Wright.
That Sunday afternoon I saw Arna Bontemps and Augusta
Savage. And Langston introduced me in New York to the
sculptor—what's the man's name?

G   Richmond Barthé?

W   Yes, Richmond Barthé.

G   *(admiringly)* Doesn't that man sculpt?

W   And he took me to his studio and I watched Barthé and
it was one of the thrills of my life.
   But, you know, I thought for my generation, for my age,
the thirties was a great decade. It was the age in which I became twenty-one, you see? And I graduated from college. I
stayed in Chicago. I published in *Poetry* Magazine. I met
other writers. How many writers did I meet in Chicago?
There were Wright and Arna Bontemps, Fenton Johnson,
and Willard Motley, Gwendolyn Brooks.

G   Margaret Burroughs was in Chicago.

W   Margaret Burroughs! I always thought of Margaret as
painter. I always forget she is also a writer because when
we met she was best known as an artist and she taught art

for many years, but Margaret is a writer. She's written several books. And Margaret introduced me to Gwendolyn Brooks. She took me to Gwen's house and Gwen and I tried to decide last April just when it was. It had to be the spring of 1938, before she was twenty-one and before I was twenty-three, so she was twenty and I was twenty-two. Of course, coming out of Northwestern [University] I renounced all my academic background and my middle-class aspirations and I tagged along with a group that was both radical and bohemian. It was an exciting time of my life—and I was writing my very best poetry.

G I know *Prophets For A New Day* was not the *worst* book that I have read.

W Well—I feel that I have some things in *Prophets*, some good things. I wrote most of *Prophets for a New Day* in the sixties. But I had started some of the things back in the forties. "Hoppy Toad" was an old poem. "Ballad of the Free" was an old poem that I finished, but it expressed better than even "For My People" so much of what I felt about black people and the whole movement toward freedom: the struggle. But I think I was really at my creative . . . not the peak, but at the beginning of my creative success in Chicago. I'd been writing all along, but I gained my control of form and my own voice there. I found my voice in the thirties.

But let's talk about the sixties. Maybe I should go back and remember that time we saw each other at that Fisk Conference in 1967.* I think John O. Killens has had a tremendous influence as a teacher of creative writing because he's been in three places where we had important schools or groups of writers—Fisk, The Harlem Writer's Guild, and Columbia.

G Yes.

*Writers' conference at Fisk University which is considered by many the wellspring of the black writing movement of the sixties.

W   And I remember first meeting Dudley Randall at that same conference. I was going to read a poem about Malcolm X, and I was sitting outside with Margaret Burroughs and Dudley came up and said there were a lot of poems being written about Malcolm and that we should collect and publish them.

G   And that was one of the first publications from Broadside Press.†

W   Yes, and I think it has developed along with black poetry much as Johnson Publications developed along with Gwen Brooks as a poet. There is also a white woman who had the same role, in a way, in the sixties that Carl Van Vechten . . .

G   I hope you are not talking Rosey Poole.

W   That's whom I was going to say.

G   Ahh, shit!

W   I know she was really trying to feather her own nest. I think it was personal aggrandizement, I agree with all of that. But she . . .

G   Ripped everybody off she *possibly* could!

W   But, Nikki, she did find a lot of black poets and published them in *Beyond the Blues*, some of which I had never heard of before. There were a half-a-dozen very good ones. People like Sam Allen, Dudley Randall, Margaret Danner, Raymond Patterson, Ray Durem. You see, not since the twenties, have we discovered so many young black voices, even if they were not so young, as we discovered in the

†Black publishing house which published many of the new black poets in the sixties and early seventies.

sixties. I have to admit to what you said, now who is this white woman coming here and, really, as you say, ripping off everybody. She said some pretty harsh things to me. Told me some of my poetry was no good and what was good and what wasn't.

G I'm perfectly unwilling . . .

W To give her any credit?

G To give Rosey full credit.

W She went to the black people and they told her who was this and who was that and where.

G And that's like if I decide I want to do a gospel album, for example. Now, if I took my tape recorder, closed my eyes and threw a map up on the wall and put some pins up and decided these are the places where I was going to go, I could come out with six sides on a twelve-side album that were excellent because the talent is there. So, I'm totally unwilling to give her credit for bringing forth a Dudley Randall or anybody else.

W Well, let's talk about something more important.

I'm interested in the differences between the generations of poets. I think about people like Langston Hughes, Arna Bontemps, Fenton Johnson, even Gwendolyn Bennet, who comes over from the twenties into the thirties, and Helene Johnson, and then my generation of poets like Owen Dodson, Robert Hayden, Gwendolyn Brooks, Margaret Danner, Margaret Burroughs, Melvin Tolson . . . In May of 1972 when we had that little workshop in Chicago, Mari Evans talked about black people and the new poetry, and I was quite taken with her name, "Our Black Family Nation," and the idea that young poets of the sixties and the seventies do not have the tendencies of the poets of the thirties and the forties to break down our society into classes and to use that Marxist angle about the class struggle. At that time we thought of all black people as being working class people and maybe now we talk about a rise of the black bourgeoisie, but Mari Evans never took that approach. It was the approach of black socialism or what do we call it, Ujamaa? Ujamaa, yes, and that's black unity, isn't it? Ujamaa, which is really African socialism in economics and politics and family relations in art and music in all the cultural phases. And that is a very distinct difference between the thirties and the sixties. Of course, in the thirties, in this country, everybody was poor. We were extremely conscious of the Depression and this continued into the forties along with World War II. It was the war that got America out of the Depression. Because things really weren't getting better.

When I compare the difference in political outlook, in social perspective, and in the poetry in terms of form and content, there are certain differences of craft and art between the thirties and the sixties. When I look at my own development, the beginning of my emergence as a poet, and compare it to those poets of today . . .

G   When did you start reading your poetry publicly?

W   Arthur P. Davis was the first person to give me a chance to read poetry at one of the black colleges. You know, he's a person that many people are not as aware of, but he is responsible for much of the work on two major anthologies, *Negro Caravan* and *Cavalcade*. Anyway, the year that I first read, 1942, was very memorable. I was going to a CLA* meeting, my first CLA meeting. I remember Frank Snowden was one of the speakers and the Rivers, both of them, were at this meeting. Oh, that was quite a collection and it seemed that the Howard men were the leaders of the CLA at that time and they treated me like a child. Nobody noticed me. I must have had on children's clothes—I was tiny enough—and I guess I looked much younger than my years. But there

---

*College Language Association.

are two or three things that stood out for me. I saw Hampton's campus for the first time. I saw Owen Dodson for the first time and he told me what I did not know—that I was winning the Yale Younger Poets Award that year. And of course I had not even submitted my manuscript and I just thought he was crazy. But I *was* winning it that year.

G   You did win it that year. That was the year I was born.

W   The year you were born! Forty-two. Forty-three is the year I married. But Arthur P. Davis invited me to Virginia Union to read "For My People." And he and Sterling Brown and Ulysses Lee, who's dead now, had asked me two years before to include it in *Negro Caravan* and that was the first time I was anthologized in any book. I never shall forget that because I never had had a poem in an anthology before then. I guess I had had some stuff in some vanity publications which I didn't realize at the time was not good to do. My mother and I submitted some poems and we had to pay for it. And once I went off to school my teachers told me never pay to have your work published, *never* do that. I learned. I didn't know. I had those pieces I had done as a youngster and in midadolescence.
    But, Nikki, when did you publish your first poem?

G   My very first poem?

W   Can you remember?

G   Yes, when I was twenty-six years old. *Black Feeling, Black Talk.* I published the whole book, if you want to call that a whole book.

W   Yeah, I want to call it a whole book.

G   Well, it just met post-office standards; it had to be twenty-four pages, and we were about twenty-six, so we made it.

W The first poems were in sixty-seven?

G Sixty-seven, I think it was.

W In five years you've come a long way.

G Thank God, huh?

(both laugh)

W It's phenomenal.

G Well, I don't consider my first book terrifically good. There were some ideas in there that I liked, but even as I published it I didn't think that it was the living end of first-poetry books. But I liked the fact that it was there. I borrowed money from friends to publish it, and I'm enough of a businesswoman to sell it once I had it. I would prefer selling it to not selling it, and the price of things like that came in. *Black Judgement,* though, I really do like as a book.

W You think it's a better book?

G Yeah. I think it's a solid book by the standards that I use. The poem "Nikki-Rosa" is in there.

W I am *crazy* about that poem. I think it's an absolutely beautiful and wonderful poem. It's a signature poem the way "For My People" is for me. I don't think you have ever written a better one.

G Well, whether I have or not, I think that one of the differences between us, generationally, is that *my* level of scholarship says that I can be wrong as long as I have enough sense to know that it can get better and to still let it go, and to go on.

W But mine doesn't allow me to be wrong?

G   No, it doesn't.

W   You're pulling my leg now. You're telling me that I have become rigid and inflexible because I insist on speaking on some things with authority. I don't pretend to know everything about anything, even about literature or writing. There are some things I do believe I have learned from a lot of experience—a long time of teaching and studying and reading and some writing. I always feel I'm more a novice as a writer than as anything else. But there's nothing wrong with my scholarship. My genius as a writer may be open to question, but my solid foundation of traditional academic education, the classicist business, that's probably where I have a kind of intellectual snobbery. I wish I were not that way; my father was that way before me and I guess I have inherited some of it. But the truth of the matter is that I have had a wonderful and very wide and varied kind of education. It isn't just from school books, it isn't just what the professors taught, because much of what they taught me I didn't believe.

G   But I didn't say anything about all that, now, Margaret.

W   But what you're saying is that when I say something, I say it's precisely that, and I hold to that point, and of course you know what that is? That's a sign of getting old and conservative and it's really the middle-age woman speaking.

G   Do you know Paule Marshall?

W   Yes.

G   O.K. Her book, *The Chosen Place, The Timeless People* . . .

W   I thought it was a marvelous book.

G   I thought it was a marvelous book, too. Unfortunately,

I didn't quite convey that when I reviewed it and there was some discussion about that. But I'm going to say something else which you can jump on me about. Paule spent, I think she said, five years working on that novel. That's too long to do anything but live.

W   Well, dear, do you realize how long it took me to write *Jubilee?*

G   Yes!

W   Half a lifetime.

G   That's too long!

W   I know it. And it's a waste of time.

G   No, it's not a waste of time.

W   I couldn't—I didn't know how, I had to learn, and everytime I put something down it didn't satisfy me. I wrote three hundred pages of that book when I was nineteen years old. I had had the germ of the idea from childhood. I wanted to write and learn how to write a novel so I could write that story, see? I lived with that story, but when I put down those three hundred pages any fool could see the thing was no good.

G   I wish I had those three hundred pages—I would read them and see.

W   But you know there were some wonderful parts in there.

G   I'm sure there were.

W   There are still sections of the final version that came from that beginning. The very first words, "May Liza, how come you so restless and uneasy? You must be restless in your mind," comes from that, in the very first draft of *Jubilee*. And the whole business of the word "wrongsiditis" that I was determined to use, "wrongsiditis," which the publishers made me respell so that people would know what I was talking about! Wrong side outwards. I had that word from childhood. I had bits and pieces. The last chapter of *Jubilee*, when Randall Ware comes to get his son and he comes back and says, "Howdy" and Vyry says, " 'Howdy yourself,' and his teeth were like the milky kernels of corn ripening in the field"—that was from the very beginning, the very first. That flogging of Vyry was in the first version. The difference was that I had carried that episode beyond the limits of the story and I didn't know the limits. I had carried it to Vyry's death at age eighty in the first version. And I remember a man telling me in 1948, "Well, you know that story really ends when Randall Ware comes back." He said, "that's the end of the story." And that was when I realized what the limits were.

But, Nikki, it is my contention and argument that many of the young poets of your generation have felt that craft, in the sense that all the schools and teachers have been talking about, is not important. I don't think this applies to you, now. It may, but I don't think it does when I read *My House* and *Gemini*. I think that the Nikki Giovanni who started out writing, say, the first things and among them the classic "Nikki-Rosa," has become even more dedicated to the craft of writing. It's very obvious in *My House* and *Gemini* that you take the craft of writing seriously. And that you work at it. Yet I believe we have had a lot of writers in the sixties mushrooming all over the country as a result more of the Black Revolution than of the Negro Revolution, who think that the only thing important is ideology or point of view. At first, there were all those poems where, as Carolyn Rodgers said, it was "nigger, nigger, nigger," you know, where you said, "Nigger, can you kill? Can you kill?" Now, she says, you've come past that to the point where you're more concerned with craft and where you're more concerned with constructing and building something rather than tearing it down.

G   I think it's all a part of the same process. You have to start someplace. I happened to have started in the sixties which is a part of that whole, as Carolyn says, nigger-nigger-nigger syndrome. I think that's correct in that that's where we were. But we have moved from that point, and to define us now as we were then is wrong.

At that particular point in time I did not say, "I am a writer." It was not until my second book that I began to say, "Well, maybe I write a little poetry." And it wasn't really until I got into *Re: Creation* that I considered myself a poet. And it is only now, and I will have published my tenth book at the end of 1973 (and I feel that ten books is a memorable achievement, no matter how we cut it), that I consider myself a writer. And if I'm going to consider myself a writer, a part of it is growth.

You know, I love plants. If you come to my home you'll see a whole window full of plants that I have begun from little seedlings. And plant life will teach you that you either grow or die. There's no static life. I like to think that I have grown and I like to think that I will continue to grow. I think that whatever contribution I may make to my people I make out of what I am inside. So, I am perfectly willing to expose a great deal of my foolishness because I don't think that infallibility is anything to be proud of. I don't believe that I should be perfect.

W   I don't believe anyone is infallible.

G   No, but I know people who think they *ought* to be, which hampers them. We can speak of your generation of writers as being like that. And this is a major difference between the two generations of writers. Ralph Ellison thinks that he ought to write another novel like *Invisible Man*. I don't think that each of my poems has to be a "Nikki-Rosa." I'm very proud of some of the foolish poems I've done or some of the love poems. I think that as a writer I simply want to continue to grow and explore. I want to get inside of people. I want to do a story on Essex, for example. Because I know that you see him one way and I see him another. And as Alexander what's-his-name-that-I-can't-pronounce [Solzhenitsyn] once said about literature, "Literature is how we communicate."

W That's right.

G   And one way I interpret that is to expose enough of myself to say, this is how I feel about that young man. I will not write a poem, "O' Essex, o' killer of white people," I won't do that. I think there is more that is important. But I do know that I need to know things, and one reason that we can sit through this conversation is that you can give a lot to me and I can take it in. Which doesn't mean that I'll just say, well, you know, goddamn, you're right.

W We don't always agree, but we can listen, anyway.

G   Not only do that, but I've found in my few years on earth that if you listen, even when you disagree, it changes you: if you just *hear* the person. Because you have to respect somebody else. I think that the writers of my generation have one terrific problem in terms of a lot of other people. It's a typical young people's problem and I don't consider myself young on that level. It's that we do not invest integrity into the people around us, into the people before us, and therefore we cannot think of ourselves as possessing integrity. If you cannot give integrity to someone it is because you do not think of yourself as possessing it.

W But, you see, you have a different concept of the word and the idea from that of *my* generation. I used to talk a great deal when I was your age and younger about a need for the writer to have integrity. But I meant a different thing altogether. I meant wholeness of personality and the integration of the personality in terms of mental and the spiritual and the physical and the social. And I remember saying I think that it takes much more than talent to be a writer, that it takes character and that you develop character. You make yourself into the person you want to be. You discipline yourself to become what you think you ought to be. If you don't have much to your personality, you can't give much to other people. Now, when you speak of investing others with integrity, each person should develop his own integrity. But when you give things—when I think of lending moral integrity to an issue—it is through your own personality and what you believe that people will want to know to respect or understand you.

G   We do mean different things.

W   Yes.

G   Because I have seen black people be so vicious with each other. And I say blacks because I don't "know" white people on that level of judging their work. . . .

W   By the strengths or weaknesses that we know in them. And that is not what we should do.

G   No, it's not fair at all.

W   A work of art should be judged on artistic standards and aesthetic standards and not on personal, moral, or social . . .

G   It must be judged on what we have, and how we can use it.

W   Well, I think, too, that it's more than this. When I read a book such as *Gemini*, your autobiographical statement, it tells me a lot about you and I may in my mind relate it to you. I may see you as I read it because I know you. But suppose I belonged to the twenty-first century, and I picked up the book and read it, because the book will be there when you are gone, and much more so when I'm gone. And the person reading it will not be able to say, "I knew Nikki." What will they get out of the book? They're going to find out what you thought, how you acted, how you talked.

G   We're going to have a disagreement here.

W   And if they don't get that from the book they have not really put their finger on the character of Nikki Giovanni.

G   But Nikki Giovanni, and I'm not a humble person, Margaret, is not the protagonist in *Gemini*.

W   You think that your little boy is the protagonist—so you think.

G   That certainly is not Thomas. It is not Thomas today and will not be Thomas tomorrow, no. The strength of *Gemini* (and I don't like to discuss my own writing on this level), but the strength is that enough of me as a writer and as a person will come through. I am my own character. Other people may use other characters. You can make Vyry your character. But that person in *Gemini* is not me. That's not my life. It's only what was useful, what I could relate to. I could write about my life from any number of points of view.

W   In other words, you treated yourself as a persona.

G   Yes, for example I read Anne Morrow Lindbergh's book—

W   *Bring Me A Unicorn.*

G   Yes. What I could get out of that book first was a period, a period of time.

W   That's a courtship period with her and Lindbergh.

G No, I didn't even relate it to Lindbergh. I mean, Charles Lindbergh is only a name in a history book to me.

W Very, very different. I was living in 1927 when you weren't.

G What I could see was how these people lived. You know, I didn't really view it anthropologically. The book expressed how they felt. I could relate what is happening to me now by those feelings. If they had those attitudes in the past, what can I expect of them and people like them in the future? You understand what I mean? Somebody, I hope—and I guess all writers or all people do—really, hope, that if a volcano erupts, my house will be the one that they dig up, and then they'll say, "This is how they lived." When they uncovered Pompeii and you saw the bread—I saw a movie on the uncovering of the ruins—you saw the bread that was baking, you saw the baby in the carriage and you say, "This is the way they lived." That's all, because Nikki Giovanni will be a name in a history book, if we're lucky. If I survive, I will be a name to those people. That's all I should be. So what you try to do is to put enough of *yourself* that is meaningful into your work. No one is totally honest about himself. No one.

W You can't be.

G You can't be that objective about yourself. Furthermore, I think I'm a nice person. I'm sure that we could go out here and find people who think I'm horrible, that I'm leading black people to ruin.

W I told somebody the other day the same thing. When I was a young woman, oh, younger than you, I was going with a fellow who was a young minister and we seriously considered marriage. I really thought I might have married him and I thought it would be a wonderful thing to marry him and I think he wanted to marry me. And then somebody told me, maybe he told me himself, that his mother thought I was a bad woman in Chicago.

G   You see what I mean?

W   And then I said, well, it would be impossible for me to understand how people would look upon me in this way. Because no woman—she could be a prostitute on Division Street—thinks she's bad.

G   That's it.

W   She doesn't think she's bad at all.

G   Of course not. And that's what I'm saying.

W   You don't judge literature on moral and social and individual personal grounds. It should be judged, for example, in terms of what this person was trying to do. What was he trying to say or what did he say? And how well was he able to say this thing? What's the psychology or the sociology? How well did he develop his characters in this story? To what extent does he resolve the conflict in this whole book? If it's poetry you've got to think about, well, what kind of form was best for him? Does he believe in a free meter, without any line or without rhyme? Does he have special devices that he uses or from where does he get his imagery— a poet doesn't write without pictures.

G   See, Margaret, we're very different on that. What I think that you get out of literature first is the strength . . .

W   I'm not talking about content and tone and philosophy.

G   Well, that's what *I'm* talking about.

W   In my book I don't see one existing without the other. The content will determine the form, not the form determine the content. But at the same time I do not see one without the other.

G You have to have form in order to have content.

W That's right.

G But you have to have a story to tell. And I don't care if it's jagged. This is difficult because I try to avoid labeling and I don't want to end up being labeled by myself in this book— but I really think that black people have got to look out for black people.

W Well, I think it's beyond that.

G I know you do. I'm just saying what *I* think. I think that the number-one thing that we do—and if you want to talk about literature, then we start with literature, though we could start anyplace—is to say O.K., if this is what we have, then what can we get out of it? And I mean that in terms of extracting its essence, its feeling, to preserve it and pass on its importance, rather than destructively criticizing it because its craft may have been imperfect.

W Nikki, and this is getting back to personalities, but I mean in terms of work, too. I can go back and remember what somebody said when *Black Fire** came out and he was talking about the people in *Black Fire* and said, "Holy smoke, how long do you think we will be reading *them*?" I said this is not the point, nobody can tell when you pick up a book how long these people's names are going to be important or who's valid and who's not valid. The point is you're interested in *seeing* what's here because we're not going to be able to judge those writers now. It takes time to judge.

G For example, when you all started publishing, say, in the

*An anthology edited by LeRoi Jones and Larry Neal which represented the writers of the sixties.

forties, we were just being born. And I think that the space in those twenty years gives us enough perspective to say "For My People" will live. You know "Middle Passage" will live, "The Strong Men Keep Coming" will live.

W What about the sixties?

G That's a problem I have with critics because it's a terrific disagreement I have with them. That instead of defining and giving life to works of art that I consider *completed* creations like the literature of the earlier periods, they spend time trading on the names of the people who are now in the forefront. It is pointless to define my worth because the minute that they do that, I have a new book. Not the exact minute, but you know what I mean. They are denying me my growth and that is unfair.

W I do not feel that that is a valid criticism.

G I do! Look, there is a reason that Shakespeare exists today and is required reading by the time you finish high school. There is a reason that you read Dostoyevsky, that you read Milton. And it's because the scholars have taken seriously their responsibility to preserve them. Blacks, too, have classics, but most of our scholars want to spend their time analyzing something that is not analyzable.

W Well, in the field of literature, I suppose the weakest part is the critical part, but we've had two or three things done there. We've Addison Gayle's *Black Expression* and *Black Aesthetic*. There's Stephen Henderson's *Understanding the New Black Poetry*.

G But I'm talking about appraisals of specific authors, appraisals which should make them classics too. For example, there's no critical book on Charles Chesnutt.

W Oh there is, there is!

G   Well, it's good and well hidden.

W   Well, that's right, you don't see it often.

G   It's this sort of thing I'm talking about. And I don't say I see every damned thing that comes along. But there is an absence of scholarship on our writers. Where are the definitive critiques of Dunbar?

W   We're getting ready to put together a Phillis Wheatley bicentennial conference at Jackson State College.

G   And that will probably be the first critical look at Phillis Wheatley on such a large scale.

W   Nikki, we are weak in criticism because we were busy analyzing white literature instead of looking at our own. But we do have to put this in perspective. For example, in America, black drama and white drama, as well as literature, comes of age only in the twentieth century. There's not much but melodrama for the nineteenth century, and in the eighteenth century America was still looking at the old country. That's why it's so important to honor Phillis Wheatley. Here's a woman in the late eighteenth century who had published a book and who had gotten notice in London as well as in this country. It's very important. But, you see, black people should be proud of that because, as a matter of fact, despite the fact that we were in slavery, white people didn't have anything more to show. They weren't doing any better and they weren't in slavery.

G   That's true.

W   Now, when I was in college the white universities didn't let people major in modern American or modern British literature. You know why? I finished college in the thirties and twentieth-century literature was still very young. You understand what I'm saying? The century, the time had not passed. We have moved toward a black literature that goes along with the maturity of the country itself and the black revolution which has occurred in the last few years. We're not behind in anything. You couldn't have a large body of criticism. What happened is that these white critics ain't been worth a damn, excuse the expression. And I say American white literature was just so much and no more. You have—if you go back into the history of American literature and take the great writers—only half a dozen or so.

G I agree.

W Criticism for us is just coming of age. It hasn't quite reached maturity. And that maturity requires time for critics to establish chronological distance from the work, so that they may be objective. For example, I'm not a natural critic, but sometimes I have some good critical insights and that's why I'm very worried now about my forthcoming book on Richard Wright. And I'm not at all sure that I can be very objective about Wright because I know so much about him and his work. I noticed that in the case of some of the things I wrote people agreed with me that they were true, and they don't necessarily tally with the comments that Robert Bone made. Bone and I don't agree on many things, yet there are some points on which we do agree. I remember when Bone was running around to blacks, including me, to get this information for *The Negro Novel.* Jerre Mangione, who did this book on the writers project,* wrote me, talked to me at length, and then I look in the book and see that he took whole passages of what I said. So, sometimes I might have some critical insights. But some of the younger black critics have the insights, but have not done the reading. I think Don Lee falls in this category.

You see, I have lived with black literature just as much with any kind of literature—white American literature, English literature, Continental European literature, and world literature—all my life. When I was eleven years old I was

*The Dream and The Deal: The Federal Writers Project 1935-1943.

reading people like Langston Hughes and Countee Cullen. I sent my first poems off to W.E.B. Du Bois at the *Crisis* and I saw him when I was seventeen years old. And James Weldon Johnson I remember as a personality, as a man, you see. It is very difficult for me to undertake literary criticism because I am familiar with a great body of literary history. And literary history is different from literary criticism. But both are important.

G I think that it's important, also, that we don't pass it off as criticism. We should deal with it for what it is, as a history and a remembrance.

W Yes. As for what I'm doing about Wright, I think I should even change the title. I said I was doing a "critical study," but I think I am too close to the man as I remember him to be a true critic.

G But it remains literary history.

W It's going to be a biography as I knew the man personally. It's got to be. And the opinions I express are not necessarily valid literary criticism.

G But it would be insightful and helpful and therefore much more compassionate.

W A man mentioned something interesting yesterday on one of the panels at the Creative Writing Conference.* Something about writing autobiography. He was talking to Willie Morris—who was his friend and not necessarily mine —and he said about his book, *North Toward Home*, "Well, you know in a book like that you have to do a lot of lying," and he added that he realized that in all autobiographical

*Conference held in January, 1973 by the Library of Congress in Washington, D.C.

writing a lot of lying is going on. And then I sat there and I thought about *Black Boy*. It's true Wright has a lot of lying in there. It heightens and intensifies what is true.

G   One cannot look at the naked truth because one does not know it.

W   And no individual is completely objective about himself. We agreed earlier that no woman sees herself as a bad woman.

Lawrence Reddick, in talking about the autobiography I am writing now, said, "Are you going to tell all that stuff back there?" It struck me suddenly that people would expect lurid passages about Margaret Walker in the thirties. And I said, "Huh?" And he said, "You know, you're supposed to." I said I'm not writing any true confessions. After all, Margaret Walker is not *really* a talker.

(both laugh)

G Let's talk about something I have been concerned about: the destructive criticism of black movies. I think the critics have been off base. *Sweetback*, for example, made eleven million dollars. First of all, we need that eleven million dollars because the same number of black people that go to the movies go to the movies whether *Sweetback* is showing or not.

W That's so.

G If they are going to go to the movies . . .

W Let it be for us.

G Let it be *Sweetback*. Let that money flow into Melvin Van Peebles' hands, who will become the first black person in modern times to run two shows that are hits on Broadway. That's what he did. *Don't Play Us Cheap* and *Ain't Suppose to Die a Natural Death*. And he is a young man. He has opened more doors than the average black man who's standing around criticizing what Melvin is doing. And I'm saying this in all sincerity, if *Ain't Suppose to Die* hadn't opened on Broadway, there wouldn't be all the colored plays you see on Broadway now. They started saying, everybody started saying, let me get a colored play in my theater. What the critics are basing most of their criticism on is if the image is positive. Image does not matter, image is not about content. Image is individualism.

W I guess some people prefer that it would have been something else besides *Bad Ass Sweetback*.

G Maybe people would have, but, goddamn, it *was Sweetback*. It has been done. That door has been opened, and to try to deny Melvin the fruits of his labor . . . you see? I don't know who Melvin sleeps with, I don't care. I don't know that he cares that I happen to love his two plays. It doesn't matter because I know when I walked out after both of them I felt better. And that's where I say that our intellectuals are corrupt. If *Superfly* does the business that it does, and the kids come out and they want to sniff up, snort like that boy snorts, it's still a black image. Rather that they want to be Priest than they want to be something out of *The Godfather*. Better Flip Wilson than Bob Hope. Certainly better Harry Belafonte and Sidney Poitier than John Wayne and Steve McQueen. John Wayne, Bob Hope, all of them will tell you they don't like black people. John Wayne already said he hates us. You see?

W I've never paid any money to go to see them.

G That's *you*. But the same number of people who want to go out of their little dingy houses . . .

W To escape.

G To escape and to have some relaxation. I used to go to drive-in theaters in Cincinnati, Ohio. I went to neck. Most people did. We didn't give a damn what the movie was. We used to go out with our boyfriends on double dates and we kissed all during the show. When the lights came on, we got up. You understand? That's what you do in a movie. So better even that *Blacula* be showing than *Son of Frankenstein*, because we know that all the money from those white movies go back to their community and is used to build their very "fine" art on.

W I see down the long road you're going. And I am saying that I will go along with all the attitudes you have brought out: the fact that we need the money in the black community, and the fact that it's good to have it in the black community. Somebody said when I was in Atlanta the other day, "If the kids like *Superfly*, let them see *Superfly*." Give them some kind of incentive or motivation so that you have something for them to write about in their schoolwork. Let it be *Superfly*, if that's what it has to be. But, I still want to come back and take issue not with the commercial success of the thing but with its artistic value. I haven't seen Melvin Van Peebles' work but I doubt that I would ever go to see that play, or that movie, it just never would appeal to me. You understand?

G   You might be very surprised.

W   I might.

G   Thomas enjoyed it. Thomas saw it with Chester Himes. And Chester is older than you.

W   Yes.

G   And Thomas is younger than anything you have walking around here, and both of them liked it.

W   Now, I *will* say this. I'm tired of hearing that everything black people do has to be morally good and uplifting, because life is not like that. And art is a reflection of life. I say that I have just as much right to write a ballad that deals with the street people and folk culture as I do to make a public statement in the tradition of the preacher, or a sermon. I have just as much right to write "Hoppy Toad" as I have to write "For My People." Both of them are reflections of what I feel is black life. So we may not always like *Superfly* or *Sweetback*. What is it, his Bad Ass . . .

G   Song.

W   Song.

G   *Sweet Sweetback's Bad Ass Song.*

W   *(chuckles)* I never can get it straight because I have such a time getting off the "Bad Ass," you know. But I still say that for my money, I want to see a certain other type of thing, too. I'm not going to say it is wrong to do this and get rid of that. I'm saying that I want to see movies like *Buck and the Preacher,* that's for me.

G The success of *Sweetback,* the success of *Shaft,* the success of *Cotton Comes to Harlem* has made it possible for you to see *Buck and the Preacher,* and that's why I get very upset with critics because they never look at the connection.

W But you see, this is another thing you are not thinking about, Nikki. This is hard for me to put into words, but I think I need to do it as clearly and frankly as I can.

G *(smilingly)* O.K., ruin my blackness.

W Black people, especially those petit-bourgeois so-called intellectuals, are terribly afraid of the image of what whites have called our maligned type. And you know, this is your prudish prude who wants to show that everything black has got to be of a certain morality. He wants to be the puritan. And it is interesting that this attitude is prevalent not only with older intellectuals but the younger ones as well, though their reasons stem from a different source.

G And what has happened as a result is that the critics and the publications they write for no longer reflect the concerns of the people. You know, you take Johnson Publications: *Ebony, Jet, Black World*—I think they have reneged on their responsibility. For there is at least an essence of truth that must be told and one would expect for the kind of pioneering that Johnson Publications did, for example, with the Emmet Till case or the Mack Parker case and some of the other unpopular cases. The reason I read *Jet* Magazine a long time ago, and I remember the Emmet Till case was one of the first times I became involved with *Jet* Magazine, was because they were reporting that this boy was missing. A body had turned up and they were one of the few publications which, horrible as it may seem, would at least show you the picture so that you would know what had happened and therefore become outraged.

W They had a picture in that magazine of the boy in the coffin, didn't they?

G Yeah.

W All swollen-up—horrible.

G Yes. And one must see that, otherwise one could say, "This did not happen." If *Ramparts* had not pictured the photographs of those napalmed children, I doubt that the peace movement would have taken the direction it did because the *fact* of those napalmed children was morally unacceptable. No one wanted to become a part of that. I mean the outcry that came as a result of seeing them. That's why I think publications like *Black Scholar* are so boring, so passionless. There are no pictures, among other things. But I've been particularly disappointed with several things about Johnson. I was disappointed with their treatment of Flip Wilson. The man has one of the top five shows in the country, which means that even an awful lot of the *Ebony* readers like him.

W What did they say?

G You didn't read that thing on Flip? and Geraldine? Didn't you read all of that? Oh, they complained that he was demeaning to the black woman.

W Well, I think I saw that, but I didn't agree with it.

G I'm saying that as the leading black publication, its own audience has already found Flip acceptable. And I would say the same thing about Lerone Bennett's article on Melvin.

W Melvin Van Peebles?

G   Yes, "Sweetback in Wonderland." I thought that it was unacceptable as a criticism of a movie, and irresponsible as a black publication dealing with a black product, because we know that *Time* Magazine is not going to hail it as the finest movie of the year.

W   Do you think it was?

G   The finest movie of the year? No, of course not, but I know that the movie made eleven million dollars, as Melvin says, "before the first white person knew it was out."

W   Tell me this, do you think that the fact that it made eleven million dollars is justification for the movie? What do you think the standards for movies should be? I hate to see black people stand up and attack black movies when we've had such a hard time getting black movies off the ground. After all, they are a *tremendous* improvement over things like *Cabin in the Sky* and *Stormy Weather*. (*both laugh*) And many of them have been commercial successes. But what about their artistic success?

G   The eleven million dollars I speak of, I speak of very honestly, because black people do not waste their money. *The Legend of Nigger Charley* did not make a fortune.

W   No. Did you like *Nigger Charley*?

G   My son walked out on it; I didn't see it. Tommy walked out on it and I figured that if Tommy couldn't bear it I would not be able to.

W   Three years old?

G   I would say, yeah. He's picky about what he watches. The *Black Rodeo* did not make money. The documentary done on Malcolm X closed for lack of an audience.

W   I didn't even know about that one.

G What I'm trying to say is that there *is* a discriminating audience, and money is one of the things we can look at, especially in terms of mass-media products. Books are not mass-media products, for example.

W No.

G Movies and records, things like that, are. One of the things we can look at is box office, to see what people are accepting and to see what people are rejecting. *Superfly* has made more money in the black community than *Sounder*.

W *Sounder* is a fine movie.

G Yes, but the point is the public is saying what they want to see and if I were a critic for a mass-media magazine I would have to ask what do they see in it. I would have to answer that they see something positive and it is my responsibility to look for that. And I'm not just talking about *Superfly*, people also like *Lady Sings the Blues*.

W I understand it's a good movie.

G I liked it.

W But I keep hearing that it is not Billie Holiday, it is Diana Ross.

G (*in a low voice*) I must say, who wants to see Billie Holiday's life?

W It was such a tragic life.

G It was such a *tragic* life. How could you film what happened to Billie Holiday?

W It was tragic, but that's what they claim to have been doing, Nikki.

G They filmed the essence and, from what I've read and heard about Billie Holiday, possibly this movie comes much closer to conveying some of her warmth. When you talk to Lena Horne or the people that knew her, they talk about what a warm woman she was, what a nice giving chick.

W Yes.

G If you just filmed what *happened* to Billie Holiday you would never see that.

W I remember hearing that record "Strange Fruit" the very year I wrote "For My People." I went to Margaret Burroughs' house and she said I want you to hear this record. I thought the thing was something tremendous. It didn't seem to me to be like a popular record. It seemed a real work of art.

G O.K., why is it real work of art—

W Couldn't be a popular record?

G Right.

W *(leaning back in her chair)* Well, now you have asked a real aesthetic question and I think a good one. Sometimes a work of art is popular. Rarely is that true because for something to be popular it must appeal to the taste of the masses, and in many instances the taste of the masses is not what we call a cultivated taste.

G *(raises voice)* But that is NOTHING BUT ARROGANCE!

W *(vehemently)* I disagree, I disagree!

G Nothing but arrogance.

W You are knocking down everything that's serious—art,

music, literature. A person like Paule Marshall, for example, that's not ordinary writing that she does. It's exceptionally good writing. And you're saying it's arrogant if everybody doesn't appreciate it.

G No, I'm saying that the fact of it's being fine means if I took *Brown Girl, Brownstones* down to my little unwed mothers in Brooklyn and read it to them, they could relate to it. They *should* be able to relate to anything that Paule writes.

W Well, now you're saying that they don't have to have a cultivated taste?

G I'm saying that art is not for the cultivated taste. It is to cultivate a taste.

W Well, I agree with that. But I'm saying to cultivate a taste is one thing, and not having it is another.

G No, I'm saying that if we are indeed as great as some-times we like to think we are, then we should be able to be heard by whomever chooses to become involved. "For My People" is a great poem, and everytime that I have heard—

W I wrote it quite by accident.

G Maybe, which is not the point. I don't care if it's acci-dental or not. If more people had accidents like that we'd be a whole lot better off. It is a poem that can be read by the scholar.

W Yes.

G It can be read by children. I can read it to somebody who is blind, you understand what I mean? Everybody from my son to my great grandmother can read that poem, and *that* speaks of art. Because you don't have to talk to me in words I don't understand in order to make your point.

W I agree. But I don't say that the thing has to be obscure. Did you ever read Joyce's *Portrait of the Artist as a Young Man*?

G No.

W There's a part in there in which Joyce talks about the aesthetic wholeness of a work; he talks about a work of art, but the standards, of course, are the ancient classical standards. He's talking about beauty and wholeness and proportion. He's dealing with what we would consider aesthetic principles. I say that is not all of it when I teach students. I tell them you have to be able to analyze a thing according to content and form. And analysis and synthesis are the two main things: taking it apart and putting it back together again. But Joyce was talking about a thing being artistically sound. I could take the naturalist's standards or the realist's standards or the romantic standards and they would all be different, but they would all end up with the same thing. For the romanticists, form isn't anything. He doesn't have to have it. Black people, most of us, are inclined to be romanticists and we have a tendency to go outside Western form and take on Oriental form. But there is such a thing as maintaining certain standards for any work of art. If you go into a museum or you go into a gallery, it doesn't matter whether you're looking at Jacob Lawrence or Matisse, you have certain things that you expect to find in a painting. You may relate to it emotionally. You see what I mean? You may relate to it intellectually.

G If I go into a museum I won't have the choice between looking at a Matisse or looking at a Jake Lawrence.

W That is all too true, but the point I'm trying to make is to enjoy great art, people don't have to be schooled in all the principles, but it meets the principles just the same.

G O. K., I can see what you're saying. We started this because we were talking about "Strange Fruit" and you said you were surprised that it became popular.

W No, I didn't say that. I said that I didn't think of it as a piece of popular music.

G But it became very popular and it became a classic.

W *I* saw it as a work of art, as a classic.

G It is a classic. And people relate to it. People related to it when she wrote it, when she first sang it. And people relate to it now.

W I think that's because of what that song is about, as much as the melody. It is all the things that are wedded together in that song.

G Have you heard Marvin Gaye's "What's Going On?"

W I think so. I think my children have the record.

G They probably do. It's a classic, too, and time will show that.

W But it doesn't move me. For example, Aretha Franklin is to you a—

G Genius.

W She *is* remarkable. But I relate better to Dionne Warwicke than I do to Aretha. That's the truth.

G   I like Dionne Warwicke, but there is no comparison. Musically speaking, Aretha Franklin is making a new statement. Dionne sings show tunes and that's fine. I do not take that away from her. I think that's marvelous and she sings them better than anybody else—"Anyone Who Had a Heart," "Walk on By." I mean, she *sings* a song. But Aretha has made another statement in terms of music.

W   Blackness?

G   No, not blackness, *music*. Just listen to what the woman can do with a *line*. The same way John Coltrane has made another statement, which tells me that everybody who comes along after Coltrane has got to take that statement into account and go forward.

W   Something *is* wrong with me. My children have tried to tell me, they try to educate me.

G   Well, that may be just an age thing.

W   I figure it's an age thing.

G   After Billie Holiday, music could not go back to Lena Horne. I love Lena Horne. But when Billie sang the way that Billie could, what she would do with phrasing, what she would do with her music, it had to go forward. And what Aretha does, what Nina Simone does, has made another kind of statement.

W   Well, Nikki, you know I just come from another frame of reference. But then I never shall forget an experience I had in the late thirties. Richard Wright and I were sitting in Frank Marshall Davis' house. Wright had taken me over to visit. And Davis used to do record reviews. He had a tremendous collection of jazz and swing and blues. He had a whole room full of stuff because he was working for the Associated Negro Press and got every record. And at the time I had not realized this was another facet of Wright—how completely entranced he was with black music. He and Davis were discussing it and got into a long discussion of swing and jive, what we called jive then. It was the beginning of what we called the hip cats, you know, and the popularity of jive swinging music, which also had its counterpart in talk and language. And I said, "Oh, it's just a fad, it'll pass." And they looked at me with my stupid self. It wasn't going to pass at all. It wasn't going to pass over.

G Not as long as we were going to be here.

W But I was still completely under the sway of my Northwestern standard English. I was unaware of the tremendous vitality of black language. I knew about black music and I always wondered whether black music was influencing me and my writing at all because I'd come to be steeped in it. I think I was extremely conscious of what I loved most, which were the spirituals. I thought I had heard every spiritual and I discovered only as I grew older that all over the country spirituals were different. That what we sang in the Deep South in Alabama and Louisiana and Mississippi were not the same songs sung in the Tidewater Country. That the people in Virginia and the Carolinas sang a different spiritual. That the people in the Georgia Sea Islands sang differently from those in the backwoods of Georgia. I didn't understand that, but I did recognize that black music was a tremendous cultural influence in the country. I knew that much, and I liked blues, too. My mother used to play ragtime. And then my sister came along playing jazz, and after that my brother with progressive jazz. Yet I wasn't familiar at that time with, say, the shouts and the hollers and the prison songs, the chain gang songs.

G I'd like to hear more about those days, especially the writers—well, you've known so many people. . . .

Notebook **IV**

W You know, it's a terrible thing, but I keep journals. I've kept diaries and journals ever since I was thirteen years old and I have boxes and boxes of them. I'm using some of them for my autobiography. I go back and read sections by the decade—the thirties, and the forties, the fifties, and the sixties.

I don't suppose I was aware of the Negro Renaissance, as such, when it was actually going on. I was too young. But at eleven years of age I saw poetry by Langston Hughes for the first time. And when I was twelve years old, my mother and father came back from summer school at Northwestern and they brought with them a copy of Countee Cullen's *Copper Sun*. But they didn't give it to me, they gave it to my sister Mercedes and brought me a book by Edgar Guest because I had been reciting Edgar Guest. I was *insulted*. As young as I was I knew that I did not have the bargain, *she* had the better book. (*laughs*) We memorized poems out of Countee Cullen's book: "We shall not always plant while others reap/ The golden increment of bursting fruit/Not always countenance, abject and mute/That lesser men should hold their brother cheap . . ." I don't remember the rest.

But I think we began reading Hughes and Cullen then, long before I saw them—I guess about four years before I finally saw Langston and much longer before I saw Countee Cullen. Before I went to Northwestern I had heard James Weldon Johnson read from *God's Trombones*; had seen Marian Anderson and Roland Hayes. In New Orleans we had heard them sing; had heard Langston; and had seen Zora

Neale Hurston without knowing who she was—that must have been about 1927. And during my first year at Northwestern I saw Dr. Du Bois, heard him read, learned everything about him. As a child, I had seen George Washington Carver in the South. My father had worked at Tuskegee when Booker T. Washington was there. He had worked in Emmet J. Scott's office and knew all about Du Bois and Washington, but was more inclined toward Du Bois. My father believed in that talented tenth business and considered that we were a part of the talented tenth. He didn't subscribe to Booker T. Washington's views. But my mother did because she went to Nannie Burroughs School for Girls in its beginning years.

G   I've heard about that.

W   It's not the same thing now. It became a training school for delinquent girls. But at the beginning it was not for delinquent girls.

G   My grandmother used to speak of it.

W   My mother went to Nannie Burroughs when she was about fifteen years old.

G   Did you ever know the novelist Charles Chesnutt?

W   No, that's really a little before my time. He died in my own lifetime but I never met him.

Sometimes in going through my journals, even with my writing about Richard Wright, I find there are things I had forgotten. I found that the title I'm going to use for the Chicago years, "If a voice speaks within you, you can live," was something he said that I had written down in a journal and had forgotten.

The same thing about Ralph Ellison. I went to New York in 1939 to a League of Writers Conference meeting. It was the year of the New York World's Fair and was the first time I saw Ralph Ellison. I put in my journal a terribly condescending remark: "I got a note from a colored chap sitting behind me who asked, 'Are you Margaret Walker?' And I said, 'Yes, who are you?' 'I'm Ralph Ellison.' " *(both laugh)* And after the meeting I was so sleepy. I had come in on the train overnight from Chicago—and was sitting in the meeting nodding, and Dick told Ralph, "Take her home so she can go to bed and get some sleep. She said she's going to stay with Marvel Cook at 409 Edgecombe Avenue." And he gave Ralph, without my knowing it, ten dollars, and said, "Give it to Margaret, I don't think she has any money." Sure enough, I was dead broke.

But, anyway, Ralph took me up to 409, but nobody was home so he took me to his own house where he and his first wife, Ida, were living, and Ida fed us lobster salad. I remember that she fixed this marvelous meal and that Ralph and I talked the whole afternoon, and, you know, I can't remember what we talked about, except I know he was talking about this book that he was working on and I keep wondering whether it wasn't the thing that he tore up and started again—*Invisible Man*—because he had such a tortuous time writing that book. But one would never know that I had ever known Ralph. I've seen him once or twice since and he always acts as if I were a perfect stranger. I remember feeling so awkward and saying, "Well it's been a long time," and something about time and changes, and he answered me rather brusquely, making me feel like a fool.

I also met Fannie, his second wife, long before she thought she would be married to Ralph. We always seemed to buy clothes that looked alike. We turned up once in the identical hat. My mother had sent me a beautiful black felt hat that turned up all the way around and had a streamer down the back like a little girl's sailor. I went to a kind of a community or club meeting or something and there sat Fannie in my hat! I nearly died.

G   I'm sure she thought, "There sits Margaret in *mine*."

W And, of course, she was a kind of a fashion plate and show person. I never was. There was always something wrong with me—either ragged stockings, or nappy hair. See, before you ever thought about a natural, the Negroes didn't speak to me because my hair was always natural. I don't wear a natural today because to me it doesn't have the same beautiful connotations. When I was a student at Northwestern, I couldn't afford to have my hair straightened so I wore it as it was and everybody said I was a disgrace to the race. My hair was never straightened. And my husband told me when we married he would always have money for two things—for me to go to the hairdresser's and to get some stockings. (*both laugh*) Of course he said other beautiful things to me besides that. When my children say, "Mama, why don't you wear a natural?" my husband says, "No, she's already had the natural days."

G Ellison appears to be kind of an enigma.

W I feel Ralph has gone conservative on art and race and moved away from a very liberal, almost radical point of view. He was never a member of the Communist Party but he published in the communist magazines and publications —in *Masses, New Masses,* many of the left-wing magazines. I never published in the left-wing magazines in my life. I suppose they didn't think my stuff was good enough, and they never wanted me.

G Well, Margaret, you were awfully nationalistic.

W Patterson* said to me in Chicago, when I tried to work on the *Record* for a while, "You don't belong here, you're a little bourgeois girl." And Wright used to emphasize the point that I belonged to a sorority, which was not true at the time, and he insisted that I was not only strongly southern, but definitely very bourgeois. That always amused me be-

*William Patterson, a black Communist Party spokesman.

cause he had bourgeois middle-class aspirations himself, though he never wanted to admit it.

G   Yes, indeed! When did you meet Gwen?

W I first met Gwen Brooks when she was about twenty years old, and I must have been twenty-two. I remember her as a very tall, thin, shy person. She was very sensitive, very quiet, and rarely smiled.

G   Have you seen her autobiography?

W I saw that excerpt in *Black World* and, I must say, I have been unable to form an opinion about it—I simply am unable to form an opinion. I'm a little startled, but I haven't arrived at any conclusion. I liked *Street In Bronzeville*. I think I must have done a review of it, and I did say that it not only showed great promise but was a very interesting and incisive picture of black life in Chicago. But *Annie Allen* is undoubtedly a masterpiece. It is a successful book in every sense of the word. It is an artistic success. Beyond doubt. It is an evenly good book all the way through and what she does there is experiment with so many different styles and forms. She even goes back to the traditional Chaucerian rhyme royal in "The Anniad," which struck me because that's a difficult form, an extremely difficult form, and I think she really worked at her craft. There's no question that she was very diligent in perfecting it.

But there have been many black writers who were very good and didn't achieve great success. So it isn't just a matter of talent. I used to say to Wright that it takes more than talent to get you somewhere. I think that in my case there's a need for integrity, a sense of character. Character is so important in consistently believing and doing what you believe in, you see, and never, never betraying your own standards or your own ideals, so to speak. You have to be true to yourself and what you believe regardless of what the world thinks or regardless of how society reacts to you. But

other factors always help. I always find it interesting that three of the forces and people who had influence on me and whom I touched were most influential in Gwendolyn Brooks' success.

One was Northwestern University, where I had a very difficult time and where only one professor believed in me. And then the man who taught me at Iowa, Paul Engle. He believed in Gwen and he takes credit for some of Gwen's success. I think it would surprise her if she knew how much Engle feels he had to do with her success. And the third person was Richard Wright. Wright got *Harper's* to publish Gwen. Harper's was his publisher and he helped her there. And a word from him really meant something. It was the same old business of the Booker T. Washington machine, where a white publishing house believed that their leading black writer is the only one who can tell them about all the other blacks. A fourth factor was the Friends Of Literature on the near North Side. Now add to that the support of Johnson Publications and you see those are the ingredients of the Gwendolyn Brooks success. I think it is a kind of phenomenon, you see, a phenomenon I haven't seen expressed in anybody's else success.

Now, I know about the ingredients of Wright's success in the same way. I know the people who got behind him. But he renounced everybody who did, black and white. The Communist Party was a strong element of Richard Wright's success and education. He got a Marxist-Leninist education in Chicago and it was the touchstone for his earliest publication and serious writing. And when *Native Son* was published, the rumor was (and how true it is I don't know) that the Communist Party put up ten thousand dollars to promote the book.

G I understand you did a lot of the research for *Native Son*.

W I surely did. I didn't do any of the writing, but, of course, people used to pass around the rumor that I wrote

Native Son. I didn't. That's not my writing at all; anybody can see that we don't write the same way. However, we have influenced each other tremendously. Look at his poems—"I Have Seen Black Hands" or "Between the Earth and Me," for example. It shocked me when I began teaching, long after I'd written "For My People," to see those poems again because he had sharply influenced me. In fact, he gave me the idea of using the forms which were *his* forms, you see. And I think it gave him great pleasure to feel that he was such a brilliant guy and that the people who had been to school were the fools.

G Let me ask you this. Are you familiar with Truman Capote's *In Cold Blood?*

W Yes.

G How would you compare the way Capote put *In Cold Blood* together with what Richard Wright did in *Native Son?* I saw many similarities. Had Wright given Capote a blueprint?

W I think I must in my own study of Wright give the analysis that I know was the making of *Native Son.* I can tell you all the ingredients of *Native Son,* because, though I don't think he ever wanted to admit it, I gave him all the newspaper clippings from the Nixon case.* But you have to go back in Wright's background, to his education in naturalism. I know people talk about Dostoyevsky and *Notes from the Underground,* but basically *Native Son* is modeled on Theodore Dreiser's *An American Tragedy*—that is the prototype. When Wright and I first met, I had already read *An American Tragedy* but I don't think I had read *Jenny Gerhardt* or *Sister Carrie.* Those were Wright's favorites. He was crazy about Dreiser and Dreiser was a writer who depended strongly upon reportage.

*A case in Chicago in which Robert Nixon's alleged murder of a white woman was transformed into a sexual crime by the police and press.

The second thing is that Richard Wright used newspaper clippings in the same way that Dreiser used the newspaper to tell the story, to help in the delineation of character. Truman Capote has done the same thing with *In Cold Blood*. As a matter of fact, many people have asked whether Capote wrote a novel or a newspaper report. The first part of *Native Son* is a reflection of sociological research that many people have been misled into believing Wright got from Horace Cayton; he didn't, he got that from me. I was writing the story before Nelson Algren or Wright ever thought about dealing with the slums of Chicago. I had lived on the North Side in my senior year at Northwestern and worked for Clifford Shaw, the Director of the Institute of Juvenile Research, and the two men who were under him, Joseph Lohman, who became sheriff of Los Angeles County, and Eustace Hayden, Jr., the son of a University of Chicago professor. Those two men were my bosses on a recreation project sponsored by the WPA on which I worked as a volunteer during my entire senior year of college. They gave me a group of so-called delinquent girls to pal around with in order to see what kind of influence a person with my background and training would have on them. They were shoplifters, prostitutes, and who knows what else? It wasn't a time when you had a widespread problem with drugs, so the two main problems were shoplifting and prostitution. Division Street was the street for prostitutes. Those prostitutes are the model for my poem "Whores" in *For My People*. The women that I saw at night with the keys jangling. They walked Division Street and that is what they did: jangled their keys. It was a kind of curiosity, especially for someone having come out of the South and a more provincial environment, to see this in Chicago. That's when I learned that prostitution and gambling were vices tied up with city politics. One of the straw bosses on the project was a man who was a pimp, his brother was a smuggler dealing in narcotics and everything.

I was so enthralled with this Italian-black neighborhood and the Project and the Institute that I decided to do a novel on it, and give it the title of the name of the neighborhood, *Goose Island*. So in 1937, the Writer's Project gave me a creative writing assignment. I was going to be paid just to sit down and write my novel! I went to see Wright the very day I got the assignment and he was home with a cold. That's when I first saw where he lived.

One of the things I mentioned in my novel was the fact that in the spring you had rat-catchers in Chicago. They came around under the Els, under the elevator trains, and in the tenements and caught rats—that big *(makes measurement with her hands)*. They had traps. The neighborhood was infested with rats. The opening part of *Native Son* deals with the big rat in the house. Now, I showed Wright sections of my novel as I wrote it. He had access to the files. He read my entire story. My research extended to Maxwell Street where the Jewish people lived. I went over and met one of the Abbott sisters* at the University of Chicago, talked to her; I did a thorough bit of research for *Goose Island*, just as I did for *Jubilee*. My main character was a woman who was very talented and a musician, but whose marriage was in trouble and who was steadily drifting into prostitution. And she ended up a prostitute on Division Street. I've always been interested in women as main characters.

In anything I write, you can expect my main character will be a woman. I'm interested in the black woman in fiction perhaps because I'm a black woman and feel that the black woman's story has not been told, has not been dealt with adequately.

Wright was working at the time on a long short story. A contest was announced for the WPA, in which I was supposed to enter *Goose Island* and he submitted four long short stories. I saw the manuscript of all those stories.

When I first met Wright, I was impressed with hearing him read his work. I was impressed with his genius and his talent as a writer. But he was still in the crude stage in that he could not spell or punctuate and he gave his things to

*Edith and Grace Abbott were American social work pioneers and lobbyists for the poor, the rights of women, and children.

me to read, revise, and type. I was just out of Northwestern as an English major and you can be certain that I could spell exceptionally well. And I taught him what to do about spelling—all the rules and how to handle them. Moreover, I typed "Lawd Today" and "Tar Baby" and the only reason I didn't type the other two manuscripts is that I was just too busy. He never paid me anything, anyway. He didn't have any money to pay with. When the contest was announced, he was preparing to go to New York. He left in May of 1937. I was still working on my novel, and did not complete it until 1939. It was very inexpertly done. I didn't understand the techniques of fiction at all and one of the editors at Doubleday (where Wright had asked the man to read my novel and probably told him what to say) said it sounded like a social worker looking down her nose condescendingly at the poor people. That shook me up. But, meanwhile, in 1938, after *Uncle Tom's Children* was published, Wright wrote me and told me he had just started this novel. I still have the letters.

Now, the body of *Native Son* is based on the clippings of the Nixon case. I must have gone to four or five newspapers. I got both the white and the black—there was the *Chicago Daily News*, the *Tabloid*, the *Tribune*, the Hearst paper, if I remember the names correctly. I sent him piles and piles of clippings, everything about the case, so much so that he told us when he came back in the fall he could put those clippings down on his 9 x 12 bedroom floor and they would cover the floor. You know how many clippings that would have had to be.

But after he had done that on the model of Dreiser, you understand, he didn't know how to resolve the book. He didn't understand the resolution, which is the weakest part of *Native Son*. That's the fault. He came back then to Chicago and asked me if I could give him a little help. He knew about the Loeb-Leopold case with Clarence Darrow. I had seen Darrow when I was twelve years old, and I went to the library and borrowed the books about Loeb and Leopold and then I reminded him that Ulysses Keys—a lawyer in

Chicago—had indicated one night at a party that whenever Wright came to let him know, he wanted to meet him. So as you see we were close on that level. Now I'm amazed these days to hear people say that I considered myself going with Wright—I never did. I was never misled about the relationship between Wright and myself. It was never what people wanted to make it out to be.

G Did you see Michel Fabre's *The Unfinished Quest of Richard Wright*, and his characterization of Wright's relationships with women?

W Yes, and it is very interesting to hear this white man expound with such seeming authority on the sexual exploits of this black man, especially his sexual relationships and affairs with black women. In view of the fact that Michel Fabre never saw Wright nor knew him personally as I did, one wonders how he speaks with such authority. It would be most amusing, even amazing if it did not immediately raise the question of his veracity. Why all this smoke-screen?

This man, Wright, seems a legendary Lothario, going from one woman to another, black and white and who knows maybe spotted? It just ain't so. Richard Wright was no ladies' man at all. All that creative energy which was mental and not physical went into books and not sexual affairs.

Richard Wright gave the appearance of an almost effete, slightly effeminate personality. He had a pipsqueak voice, small and delicate hands and feet, smooth face with very light beard, and rather fastidious ways or mannerisms. He certainly did not exude a strong maleness nor masculinity. Perhaps this is one of the answers to his problems with women. Because he definitely had problems in this area. He was intensely shy and naive where women were concerned. I venture to say he did not have an affair with any of those black women Michel Fabre mentions. As for Jean Blackwell Hutson, whose beauty Wright admired and raved about, when we compared notes she was the same kind of "blind" and "front" I was. They went occasionally to the

theater together but there was never any question of marriage or intimate physical relationship, not so much as a
goodnight kiss, never, not ever.

My own mother chided me afterwards by saying, "Anytime a man takes up your time for three years and doesn't
so much as kiss you, you know he has no romantic interest
in you, so why bother with this man so long?"

Nobody, but nobody ever could understand this friendship and the more I declared it was platonic, political, intellectual, and literary, the less anybody believed me. I must
confess I was young. He was young himself and I was seven
years younger. You see, Wright talked to me as he could
never talk to anybody else about anything—about books,
people, everything—and we talked for hours *all* the time.
We were always happy to see each other and he'd sit up in
my house till two o'clock in the morning talking.

But Wright was ambivalent toward black women. He told
me if he ever married, he'd marry a white woman. He also
said black women don't do anything but pull you down
when you're trying to get up. I said, "Now, listen, I hope
that when you get ready to marry a woman, the woman you
want to marry will want to marry you, because the most
important thing in marriage is for two people to want each
other. It's no good if I want you and you don't want me or
you want me and I don't want you. It's got to be mutual and
I hope that you will be happy with whomever you marry
and that you will make her happy. But don't talk to me about
black women, man, because I'm black." ("Negro" was the
word then.) And I added, "So was your mama and your
grandmama." He said, "All right, don't put me in the doz-
ens." You see, there I was busy helping the man all the time.
I wasn't pulling him down or kicking him at all.

But back to Fabre, it is the same old story told by white
people in our society of how morally bad black women are,
especially educated black women, and how ideally good and
pure blonde and blue-eyed or auburn-haired, hazel-eyed
white women are. That is pure mythology! What men won't
do to women in this man-oriented society! Especially to

black women! Maybe he doesn't exactly spell it out but the implications are there, the class-hate, and the race-hate.

Fortunately for me, the main thing Wright hurt was my intellectual pride, which as you know is a great sin to possess anyway. He made a fool out of me! He used me, not only to help himself as a writer, but as a blind to fool others about his complex nature and personality.

Now, when I hear how Wright had all these passionate affairs and mistresses and how many women he jilted and disappointed I think I must be reading some kind of fairy tale. I surely don't know anything about his sexual fantasies nor who was in them, and maybe Michel Fabre has some knowledge about them and does know, but believe you me, all this talk about Richard Wright's sexual prowess with women strikes me as downright phony. It is quite true he was many different things to different people. His conversations with women were obviously different from those with men, but as Arna Bontemps recently reminded me, Dick Wright was a very ambivalent man. I know we *did* talk about literature and politics. Insofar as my indiscretions are concerned, I suppose that is Fabre's side of the story. I will not dignify that with remonstrance. My story is that I was insulted in New York by Wright when he thought I was stranded without money or friends (I did have my ticket home) and he no longer needed me to help him with his novel. That is when he "withdrew."

Yes, he often spoke out against homosexuality and homosexuals who were mutual friends, but he never, no never discussed that most interesting deviate, the bisexual. I don't know whom he hated most: homosexuals, heterosexuals or bisexuals; but he hated, oh he hated, and sometimes I am sure he hated his own black self! Marriage between us was never a physical possibility. Such a marriage would have been most unfortunate for me in every sense. As I told him (maybe that was one of my indiscretions), I was always looking for a *real man*.

G What happened in New York?

W Some mutual "friends" told him some kind of lie. They said that I had said something. I don't know what they told him, but he became inarticulate with rage. They sat down one night and talked to him for hours. When I got out of the show that I had gone to see, *Abe Lincoln in Illinois*, and came back home about midnight, ready to go to bed, he rang the doorbell. "Mr. Wright to see Miss Margaret Walker." I said, "At this time of night, I'm ready to go to bed." Wright said, "I know you're not going to bed this early." I insisted, "It's time for me to go to bed—I'm tired." But he came up and then he would not sit down. He said, "Let's go downstairs." I asked, "At this time of night?" I said, "You're a little short, what's the matter?" "Search your conscience and you'll know the answer," he snapped. "What is wrong with you?" I asked. "I think you ought to go home, go back to Chicago. I don't want any scenes," he said. My mouth fell open. I said, "You mean move away from here to the 'Y' or something?" "No, I mean go to Chicago, go home, get out of here." I said, "But what about that novel?" "I'm not interested in your novel anymore— the relationship is over." I said, "Where are those people? I'm not going away from here under any cloud." "Now, Margaret, you'd better not. Don't start anything with me and don't you follow me. I'll call the cops to you." I never had anybody put a knife in me like that before. I had never followed after that man, never cultivated him a minute. He needed *me*, see?

G Was that the last time you saw him?

W You think I was gonna see him anymore? I went home and sat down. I stayed up—oh, at first I was so hurt. Then I made the mistake of going back around to the hotel where he stayed and he saw me. "I'm sorry you came around here," he said, and I said, "Well, I thought I'd come around and find out what charges you have against me so I would know what this is all about." "Don't you bother me, don't you bother me, don't you bother me," and he lit out and ran. I turned around and went back where I was and I was so disturbed I didn't sleep. I thought it was the end of the world. I just figured, here I am in New York and I had come basically because he had begged me to come and I didn't know anybody and I was even in a house where he had gotten a place for me to stay, and I didn't have any money. I stood in front of an open window eleven stories high and looked down at the ground and said to myself now, you can't kill yourself 'cause that would be foolish. Nobody knows, your family doesn't even know you're in New York. Now, how would it make sense? And then it would seem as if you had done something incriminating, or something wrong, as if you were guilty of something. So you can't kill yourself, you've got to live.

I sat down and cried.

G Did you ever find out why he was angry?

W Fabre told me just last year. He said, "Don't you know that those people in New York told him some awful things they said you had said about him. And it turned him livid with rage. And he believed you were ganging up on him." You see the paranoia, he had it. I said the thing that always bothered me was that if he could believe anybody against me and what they said, it was time for the friendship to end, anyway, and that's what I told him in a letter.

But you know he did some strange things. One time we were in front of the New School For Social Research. The white girls rushed up and said, "Oh, Dick, is this your wife? Introduce us, is this your wife?" And he just beamed. Indignantly I said, "Tell them I am not your wife. Tell them I am not your wife." But he said, "Hush, don't say anything." I asked, "Why would you have them believe that?" You see, he had a white woman there that he wanted to marry and he wanted to upset her and make her jealous and he succeeded.

G You know Richard wrote in one of his short stories—

I can't remember which one right now—that the hero
wanted to marry this "bourgie" girl and her family didn't
approve.

W It never was me. A friend told me that there was a
girl like that in his life. He didn't like any woman that looked
like me. I didn't have the kind of features he liked. If he
took out a black girl, she had to be what he called "white
pretty."

Fabre told me that Wright eventually found out the truth
and Wright wrote me. I had written him a letter in that same
first twenty-four hours—a long letter telling him I was very
sorry he'd gotten any false notions about my attitude toward
him; that I had always admired him and respected his personality and that if I had ever acted oversentimentally or
like a schoolgirl having a crush I was also sorry; and that I
promised him I would never ever bother him in any way
again, that so long as I lived he would never hear another
word from me—goodbye and good luck. And God is my
witness that I never spoke to him or wrote him another line.
But he kept every letter I had written. And his wife and I
have had this hassle with her trying to get my letters and
my not giving a damn about giving her those letters. I know
what I wrote him and there's no line of love anywhere. I
know that she can't make anything out of those letters because she doesn't know what he wrote me. There's no love
in them, either. You see? Anyway I'm not about to give
up the letters to her or any other white person. Margolies*
has asked for the letters and I wouldn't respond to him
either.

Wright was writing to me until about two years before
his death. I think his last letter came about fifty-seven or
fifty-eight. He asked me for permission to use "For My
People" in *Listen, White Man*. He sent word by people
like E. Franklin Frazier, but I never answered a single thing,
never said another word to him.

*Edward Margolies, author of *The Art of Richard Wright*, a critical
analysis.

Well, Nikki, that about tells that whole story in a nutshell. I took Wright to Keys's office and asked Keys myself for the brief he had written on the Nixon case so that Wright would have a model to write the story—the lawyer's case in *Native Son*—and that is what he used. Now I've told you the whole story of *Native Son*. That's the whole book.

G Do you think he was murdered?

W I'm not sure about that. I don't know a lot about the circumstances—I've heard a lot of hearsay. I do know what St. Clair Drake has told me, and I have his interview with Cayton in which he says that on the day he died George Padmore's widow went to the Embassy office in Ghana and said she couldn't understand why they hadn't said anything about the death of Richard Wright in the paper. She had written a story and she wanted it printed and if they didn't she was going to leave the country. Her husband, George Padmore, and Wright were good friends; so were Nkrumah and Wright. And Nkrumah and Langston were at Lincoln University together. I've often wondered if Langston didn't introduce Nkrumah to Wright. I've often felt that that's where the relationship was, because the connection was with Langston and Nkrumah from Lincoln days. And when Nkrumah became the Prime Minister of Ghana and Ghana declared its independence, Langston went over there and stayed about a year. He put in two or three years altogether in Ghana during Nkrumah's time there. He stayed in Africa a very long time and collected material for two or three anthologies, so he got to know most of the writers that were prominent in Nigeria and in West Africa. I imagine he went to East Africa and as far south into South Africa as he could because he knew many of them.

Anyway, St. Clair Drake said that they listened to Mrs. Padmore and the thing was published, but they couldn't afford to say that he had been killed.

G Before we leave Wright . . . The point I was trying to make earlier about him—whom I did not know, could not have known—that we should not be concerned . . .

W About his life but about his work?

G No, not that. It's that you brought out something else about Richard Wright, which is that as we deal with him and his work and as a man, we have to deal with that whole spectrum of his life. Now, whether or not he loved Ellen Wright because she was white or whatever, the fact is he didn't know how to get rid of her. He finally got rid of her in the only way possible for him which was that he was killed or he died.

W Now I know the thing that bothers me about the death story.

G What?

W I remember when I saw the picture flash the morning I heard he had died. I sat down and trembled. It upset me. It was one of those days, but just one day. When I went to school that day, John Eubanks said to me, "I heard about Wright. What do you think happened?" I said, "They say it was a heart attack, but I'm sure it was his stomach because he always had such a delicate stomach." He always had a nervous stomach, his nerves were in his stomach. I fed him too many times not to know that. He always ate lightly and it was simple food he needed. And he used to talk about how I cooked and all that type of thing. But I read the story of his death in *Ebony* and shortly after that I got a Christmas card from Langston that said, "I must have been the last visitor that Richard Wright had. I saw him just before he went to the hospital, and imagine my shock when I got to London and saw the papers, that he was dead." Now, I have had trouble with that. I've had trouble with three of the death stories. The story in *Amistad*, the story in *Ebony* Magazine, and the story in Constance Webb's biography of Wright. Those stories do not dovetail. There is a discrepancy of a day or two that nobody ever accounts for. Some people say he was in the hospital five days and some say he was there three days. Some say he had been sick a week. Langston said he saw him the night before he went to the hospital and told me to imagine his getting to London and seeing the papers and reading that he was dead. That couldn't have been as many as five days. You see what I'm saying—there's a discrepancy somewhere in the reports that I have. I didn't think of foul play until I read Constance Webb's book. What is the date of her book? Is it 1968? It's after I went to Fisk. The first time I heard any report that he had been killed was at Fisk, when someone said, "Oh, you know that woman killed him." I have been amused because all of these different cases add up to the fact that the French government was not pleased with him, the American government was not pleased with him, that the Communists were not in love with him.

G   That he supported the independence of Ghana and Algeria.

W   He was known to give information to certain African governments. It was a game of intrigue. I don't know how much money he was getting out of it, if any. I know it must have entertained him greatly. But when I read this woman's book, was the first time that I saw with my own eyes what had happened to the man. And I do not buy the story that the CIA killed him, even though John A. Williams implies that he was killed by them in *The Man Who Cried I Am*.

G   Somebody was behind it.

Chapter **V**

The Last War

W Do you believe that the white man will succeed in destroying all the black people in this country?

G *(in a slow deliberate tone)* From what I have seen— and I'm not just talking about the camps created for the Japanese, or even just the dope by itself, though dope is *definitely* a part of it because the need for dope has led to an increase in violence and crime—it's the violent crime that is the major threat. The crime is unacceptable, not only because of what it is doing to our community, but because it is an invitation for the police to come into the community and commit violence upon us.

Now, in major cities you're used to being robbed, you *object* to being killed! I've been robbed, it's no big thing. I'm saying that given that and the dope-crime syndrome, which centers on the most vital part of our community—our young black men—it makes a very serious situation. No race survives without its young men.

I remember some time ago Percy Sutton* held televised public hearings on crime. They were held at one of the churches there. The people who got up to testify were mostly black men and women sixty to eighty years of age, and younger black women.

W It was happening to their children?

G No, I'm talking about the victims of crime. Most of them

*President of the Borough of Manhattan, New York City.

103

were saying that they could not walk the streets because they were being mugged by younger black men, our teen-aged hoodlums. In Newark there was a terrible case where three black men repeatedly raped an eighty-year-old wom-an, hit her on the head and killed her. That's unacceptable, not only because of the crime itself, which is despicable enough, but because it would please the Governor to have an excuse to "clean up" Newark.

W Yes.

G Another thing we're seeing today is lack of concern for the dope addict because he is an "offensive" dude. And somehow or another that must stop.

W This is the reason that there is not as much concern as there should be. When I think about my own feelings and my own fears and my own terror of the addict it is because I think, as my son says, most people have very little real specific knowledge about the drug addict, that drug traffic or the dangers of it or how much has been blown up. How much is real and how much is not real?

G I was reading an *American Medical Association Journal.* It was talking about the increase in reported overdoses, O.D.'s, yet death in most cases was instantaneous. That means that they were not O.D.'s. Now, the AMA is conser-vative and cracker and I had always said that it's almost im-possible to die of an O.D. unless you're shooting-up alone and nobody's around.

W And nobody can get to you in time.

G Exactly. Most drug addicts shoot up in groups. In most of the "O.D." cases, the needle has not been pulled out of the arm, which means death was instantaneous! But with an overdose you die because your vital organs slow down until they can no longer function. Your lungs slow down, oxygen doesn't get to your brain, you pass out, and you die. So these instantaneous deaths are not O.D.'s.

G   Well, why is it happening so many times?

W   It's something in the drug. Now they say it may be the amount of quinine that gets mixed with something else. There's something in the drug that causes instant death.

W   Now you're saying that the drugs are delivered poisoned to kill the people.

G   You see, I can't say that for a fact—I can't say that they're putting poison in it.

W   One thing I learned when I was nineteen in Chicago was that there's no way in the world that a gangster, a criminal, or any organized syndicate can carry on illegal activities —whether it's narcotics, liquor, prostitution, gambling, or any vice operation—without the protection of the police and the involvement of the city, state or federal government. If the government wanted to they could control and destroy the drug traffic. Therefore, they must be earning money from it.

G   A lot of money.

W   Even the most naive person understands that this has got to be a related thing. And Dick Gregory, I guess, was the first one I heard say, "My little nine-year-old boy knows the pusher. You mean to tell me the policeman can't find him?" In other words, this country has a spy and a Gestapo system. They can do anything it wants them to do. I shouldn't say Gestapo, I guess. That's not the word.

G   It'll do. Pretty soon it will be a *mild* word.

W Of course, my sons say that the Vietnam war has been perpetuated as a means of destroying young black men, that more black men were being killed because so many of them were over there. More of them put into it. As the men constantly say, they were given the most dangerous jobs to do; they were put on the front lines. They were sent down in the bush and kept down there for months at the time and they were fed the dope, they were deliberately given the dope.

G And your sons are rural.

W Rural?

G Yes, as opposed to urbanized.

W You consider Jackson rural?

G Compared with New York, yes.

W *(laughs)* Isn't that wonderful!

G O.K. Maybe I've offended you.

W No, I'm not offended, it's just that it looks more rural to you.

G O.K. If they took as many of the black men percentage-wise out of Jackson as they take out of Harlem, they would be missed. It would be a drastic change.

W You see, from Mississippi they were sending so many black men to Vietnam—eighteen- and nineteen-year-olds, the last males of the family—and so many were coming back in boxes in a matter of six weeks to six months that there was a real protest.

G   That's just what I'm saying. When you miss them, you can protest; in a city the size of a New York or the size of a Philadelphia or the size of a Chicago; you don't miss the same number in terms of the number of bodies. It's even more, but they're not missed in the same way.

W   Now let me ask you this. You were here when I said the prisons were going to explode, a year before Attica even happened. I know that something's going on in those prisons. And the men are aware of what is happening. That's why you're getting so many absolute outbreaks.

G   Trying to bring attention to it.

W   They're full of black men all over this country.

G   There's a tremendous gap on the streets of that seventeen- to thirty-year-old male.

W   Yes. Three things have always been true in the South where the black male is concerned. When he's seventeen years of age, eighteen at the most, he's going to be one of three places: in the army, in school, or in jail. At that age he hardly has a job. A very small percentage of young black males can be found working on jobs profitably—who are not in school, not in the armed services, and not in jail. That has always been true for young black males in the South. I think it's true now in all the big cities.

G   Right, and the ones you *do* see are what a lot of people would call offensive.

W   I was very interested in something that Andrew Young said in Atlanta in April, and I was so glad to see he had won because I believe he will make a good congressman from Georgia.

G I hope so.

W He said at a luncheon that he was concerned about where the unemployed are. He said you read about unemployment and you know that the unemployment figures are up, particularly among black people. He said during the Depression you saw unemployed men standing around on street corners. You don't see them now. I guess you do in the big northern cities.

G Who doesn't see them?

W You don't see them here.

G We do.

W We don't see them standing out on the streets and I didn't see them too much in Chicago. You probably see them more in Harlem than anywhere else. I do remember that during the Depression you saw men in the streets loafing, without work. You saw them sitting down on the street corners, you just saw lots of people. But now, in most of the cities that I have been in, you don't see them as you saw them then. I began to wonder where these people were and I discovered that there is a whole new economy based on crime and drugs. There's a whole new economy. For instance, the thieving rings operate from city to city. The people who break in and rob and take whole houses of furniture away, they just pull a truck up to your door. This is a different kind of thing. They don't intend to kill anybody; they don't have to shoot anybody. They go when the people are not at home and take everything out of their houses and then they move it to another city and sell it. It's a whole organized ring. A whole new economy based on crime and drugs. You see? But the guy who's an addict needs a quick money turnover with the sale of a small appliance or something. That's the only way he can support his habit.

Now I was interested in that because you have a different kind of situation with the streets from what we formerly had, and, as we said, all seems to be tied in with the city, with politics, and with government.

G I would agree that there's a big difference between what happened in the Depression and what's happening now. The Depression was the first time people were out of work, historically.

W Oh, no. You had had panics in the country before.

G Yeah, but they were very different in terms of scale, in terms of the fact that the people kept hoping that work was going to come back.

W Hoover kept telling us prosperity was just around the corner, just like now with Nixon: Peace is just a day or so away.

G But what you have now is a group of men commonly called the permanently unemployed.

W Yes.

G And naturally you are not going to see these people standing in lines, because they do not consider their situation temporary.

W Soup kitchens and bread lines are not there.

G They're not there because these people are permanently unemployed and have been out of work almost all of their lives. We have second- and third-generation welfare recipients.

W I understand that.

G   So, of course, they are not standing in a line waiting for a handout or looking for a job because they already know...

W   That there aren't any jobs for them.

G   Sure. You saw all those white guys and black guys lined up in the Depression asking for work. A man who has been out of work since he was twenty-one or twenty-two who is now thirty or forty is not going to stand in a line. And his son is not going to stand in a line, either. That's why you don't see the groupings. I don't know where Andy's been—I can't respond to his specific experiences—but I have been in Chicago, in Los Angeles, and of course, in New York where I live, and when I have been in Atlanta, I have seen scores of people...

W   Standing on the streets.

G   Standing on the street corners. Not in groups of twenties and thirties, but in groups of twos and threes. You see the black guys, the young black guys, with their collars zipped up, going down the street together. I recognize them all as part of the permanently unemployed because during those hours of the day you know that they should be working.

W   I think I understand what has happened and much of it is due to the electronic revolution. Mechanized farming, for example, has cut all the black people off the farms in the South and sent them to the cities where there are no jobs, sent them to the welfare rolls. And then there are all the people who have been thrown out of work in the cities because of the machines taking over the work of so many people. I suppose once upon a time we talked about the problem of leisure, that you don't have to have guaranteed employment for the whole society. But what do you do with all these unemployed people who don't expect to work anymore, who are not going to school? If they are not going to be caught up in this economy of crime and drugs, what happens to these people?

G You know, I don't believe that your average addict—the addict's addict—is in a ring.

W He really can't function physically well enough.

G He's not functioning at all. The ring is being run by very straight, very functional guys who could be placed tomorrow on the stock market. The numbers racket is being run by some of the most brilliant guys in the world, barring none. I would put him up against any cat on the stock market because he knows what he's talking about. Of course, numbers has become almost legitimate, and eventually it will be because it is such big business they no longer wish to consider it illegitimate. But I'm not complaining about numbers-runners. The South has always been noted for them. I lived up in Knoxville, Tennessee, and there the biggest men in town were numbers men and it was respectable. I am complaining about violent crime and I'm complaining about the fact that groups of men are now continually coming up who are experiencing no gainful employment. They are not finding that they are worth anything. And I think it is for us to create that worth for them as a community. We must find out what we want to do with our young men, because we are not doing it now.

W Does that mean that we need to re-examine the uses of education and the kinds of education that we should have in our society?

G We need also, and more importantly, to re-examine what makes a person, what makes a man and what makes a woman.

W You mean getting away from the whole business of role-playing in society?

G Role-playing is not good because it is not working in our community. For example, a lot of professional white men now find themselves unemployed. They are very upset. In New Jersey the news just recently featured one of those aeronautics-engineer-type people who has been unemployed six months. Well, his wife is still working and what this man has done—which I personally thought was so fantastic—is simply take over the house. And they asked him, "How do you like it?" and he said, "Well, I'm not *terrifically* fond of the role I now find myself in, but it's good to get to know the kids, it's good to get to understand something of what my wife was going through and I think that we are going to hang in there and we're going to pull on through." Now maybe that's an exception. I know too many editors, for example, who are tending bars in New York City because publishing houses began to close and to combine. Many senior editors found themselves out of work. Men cannot let a genetic, physical presence which says, I am a man, therefore I cannot stay home and fix sandwiches for the kids, keep them from being functional.

W There's a change in the whole role of the family.

G A change in the way the male performs, a change in how we look at the female. And there is a change that I feel is obviously necessary, because if we don't use our energies positively our energies will be used negatively.

W I agree with that.

G And I think we have to get rid of those sex-derived roles that have nothing to do with modern society as we know it. If a man has not worked for the last ten years, or the last five years, or even, I would say, the last two years, the chances are he is not ever going to work. And I believe that our children who are coming up under that situation will be very different, because they see in order to be a fulfilled person you must do what is necessary, regardless of predetermined roles.

W Yes.

G Have you been to Africa?

W No.

G You must go. You talk to any number of tribesmen and you say, "What do you do?" They'll say, "My tribe is a warrior tribe. We are fighters." Then you'll ask, "When was the last war?" and they will say "four hundred years ago." I'm not kidding. I met tribesmen in Ghana and all over and they said, "We are fishermen," and I would ask, "What do you do now?" and they'd say, "We haven't fished in over a century." We as a people cannot afford that fantasy. You understand? We cannot afford that fantasy. My man will say he is a carpenter and you ask when was the last time you made something? Ten years ago? You are no longer a carpenter and you must find something else to do. You cannot cling stubbornly to something that used to be. You must move into what is. Because we find that our young men and young women need the input of these people, the positive input of these people.

We're talking about the muggings and things, about community control. There are many things to be done but nobody wants to do them because they say, "I am not that."

W Yes, but there would be something else.

G No there wouldn't either because you're the kind of woman—and I am also—who writes poetry. I would do something else. But most people would say, "I am a school teacher, I would not bake cakes for a living." You understand what I mean? And we can no longer think that way. If there are no more schools to teach in, we do something else that is a life-force and we move on. And too frequently our men are not moving, and if it is a complaint against black men, I'll accept it as such. Our men are not moving in the direction of fulfilling the needs that we see expressed every day on the streets. The happiest times I felt about black men coming into themselves, if I may say so, were during the riots.

W Yes.

G Which everybody complained about. But I saw that they got together and I would say that I as a woman—I was a younger woman then—saw that they got together. They decided that the situation was not bearable and they said we will fight. We will fight with what we have, however we can, but we will fight. And from that point on you began to see a lot of assassinations of key political figures. And you began to see the repression of the black community, and the jails fill up, and the emergence of the Panthers— from the point when those men got together. And I say this is no time for us to separate.

W And the proliferation of the events since the riots should be a cause of great alarm. This country with its elections in 1972 reached the same point that Germany did in 1932. I am sure, I am very sure, that what has been happening on Southern's campus is only the beginning and that what is happening in the navy with the racial incidents is only the beginning. What has been happening in the prisons is not over. What is happening with the desegregation of the schools all over the country is not over and Nixon is getting ready for just what John A. Williams called "a national emergency of black violence and racial incidence." Now it is going to be difficult to survive a thing like that. If you live completely on the negative side of it the paranoia can immobilize you. So you have to have the kind of faith that is constructive and, as you say, believe in the feeling among black people that binds us together because of our common problems.

G And our common joys.

W Yes.

Chapter **VI**

In/Conclusion

W I was thinking at dinner about two revolutions, the Negro Revolution and the Black Revolution. In the late fifties and early sixties we had a half-dozen black civil rights leaders. Men who have vision, who had purpose, who were able to use effective tactics and who got out in the street and accomplished something. It doesn't seem like much because it was primarily public accommodation and transportation and voting rights. And then integration of jobs through economic boycotts and marches. You know, you can go anywhere in the country now from Jackson, Mississippi, to New Orleans, to Chicago, to New York, to Philadelphia—anywhere—and it's nothing to go into the stores, certainly in the black community, and find a black clerk and cashier. You simply never had that before the Negro Revolution. You just didn't have it. Now, then there came the cry that this was just for the middle-class Negro. He's the one who can go to the motel and afford to get a room and who needed the overnight accommodations when he was traveling. And it was for him who used the first-class accommodations on the train, for example. (Of course, I associate the deterioration of the trains with racial integration.)

But the Black Revolution did something else for black people. And I think that black men got a shot in the arm from both. In the first revolution we had that educated black man, that black Baptist preacher, capturing the imagination of the masses of the black people by harnessing the emotional drive of religion and the black church for the purpose of political activism and achieving civil rights. We were

117

working toward voter-registration drives and economic boycotts and marches and using the tactics of a Gandhi and even some Marxist tactics—using all these with great imagination, skill, and effectiveness for approximately ten years from 1954 to 1964. Then you have immediately after the death of Malcolm the beginnings of the Black Revolution. And this was a revolution of the minds—to change the minds of black people about themselves. All the problems of identity and alienation and the self-concepts of the child. Then it was a revolution in dress and in hair styles, revolution in terms of a sense of pride and beauty—all of that. The Black Revolution was tremendous because it offered to give back to black people manhood and womanhood, such as the Negro Revolution did not do. The Negro Revolution was demeaning in that blacks continued to accept all kinds of abuses. The men let the policemen step on them and step on the woman's neck. The Black Revolution was not that kind and I think that's when your riots really began, about 1965. You had Watts and from then on through the time of King's death in '68. For about three years you had rioting. I guess the climax came with the Chicago trouble during the Democratic Convention. But that's when black people recognized that what they were dealing with in terms of repression was absolutely death-dealing and genocidal. I think that in '69 after the first hundred days, Nixon began his campaign of repression against black as well as poor people of *all* kinds. . . .

G And young people.

W Yes. In 1970 they tried to kill three movements at one time. I don't think they completely destroyed them but they attacked the student movement, the peace movement, and the black Poor People's Movement. The government attacked all three in 1970. But they began in 1969. And it was 1970—all the summer of '70—that we saw the attacks on black people in the community which have not stopped since. Supposedly, at first, it was a shoot-out with the Black Panthers. And then they were getting rid of the RNA. Next they talked about these militant blacks in Harlem and in Florida and all over the country and this went on for almost all of Nixon's first term. Now what can we hope for in a second term if this is what happened in the first term? We can expect it to be worse.

G Yes, I think it's going to be worse. But, again, I think it's up to us. We were very late in recognizing that the attacks on the Panthers, for example, were simply attacks on black people, essentially black men. But we would debate their philosophy. When I talk about the corruption of the intellectual, that is what I mean. We would debate if the Panthers hadn't said this and hadn't done that then nobody would have moved against them.

W That wasn't true.

G The intellectuals debated things that were beyond debate. The thing that has depressed me most about them was their inability to defend Rap Brown—their lack of interest in defending H. Rap Brown and their hatred of that movement. But those first two things, especially, were crucial issues in terms of the black community. Whatever Rap Brown is, he belongs to us. He came out of Baton Rouge. He went to Southern University. He went to Washington. He went to live in New York for a while. He followed the student movement. He came up through black people. There was no white intellectual anything supporting H. Rap Brown. He may have been intensive, he may have been offensive, he may have made many mistakes, but he belongs to us as no other person has belonged to us that has risen to that particular national level. He was our creation. He was a creation of the people.

W How much of the business of arresting Rap Brown and the so-called robbery was a frame-up, in your estimation?

G   A great deal. And of course they must surely have known where Rap Brown was all the time. They shadowed everybody. They came by my house regularly to the point where I could say, "Oh, the FBI is by again today. What can I do for you gentlemen?" You know I'm serious about that. They shadowed all the people who ever *knew* Rap. So I'm sure that they knew where he was almost all the time, *'cause a nigger that tall can't hide anywhere.* And you figure if Angela Davis can't get out of the United States, Rap Brown sure as shit can't hide in New York City.

W   You think Angela at the least was trying to get out of the country when they got her in New York?

G   No. She was trying to be arrested in New York. The chances of being shot down are slimmer there.

W   My neighbor asked me what I thought about her arrest. I said, "Well, I wish she had gotten out of the country. I wish they hadn't caught her. God knows what they don't mean to do to her." And my neighbor said, "Yes, all of us, if-push-came-to-shove and she came to our door tonight, any black woman worth a dime would hide her."

G   That's right. Because everybody, for whatever reason, would identify with Angela. Now we're talking about a problem I am obviously pursuing rather closely. This is not true of black men.

W   You mean they don't feel that way about each other?

G   Nobody feels that they feel that way. Rap Brown was arrested because someone told where he was.

W   Had to be.

G   Exactly. Only three people knew where Rap was and

none of them was his wife. You understand what I mean? Some black guy . . .

W Had to.

G At least that's the feeling one gets. I'm not accusing anyone. The point is, though, that the thing which saved Angela Davis, for example, that saved Huey Newton, and may still save Rap Brown, is the level of concern that is an across-the-board people show.

I just wrote a letter to the *New York Times* because they printed a horrible article on Coretta King. I've never written to the *Times* before in my life. But I had to protest.

W What did they have to say about her?

G That she was a black Jackie Kennedy. And that she was a snob and didn't really want to be black, that she really wanted to be a white woman. It was just a snide put-down.

W That's terrible.

G The point is that if they can put down Coretta King in November, Nixon will have free reign on Martin King by January.

W I have never felt good about Nixon in the second term. I feel that the kind of vote they claim he got is simply to make it possible to set up real military dictatorship in this country.

G I agree.

W That is what he envisions. I think that in this case of a man who is nearly sixty years of age. And anyone who has been doing the kind of ego-tripping this man has been doing for the past four years, talking about himself as the

President of the United States and acclaiming himself over and over again over the house of cards—a man who from the beginning has been supported by the country's chief industrialists, by the whole military industrial-complex, by the World Bank; a man who was put in the position purely by money, four hundred million dollars spent to buy the position—there is nothing this man cannot be paid to do. He has been bought and paid for. He has got to deliver and in this country paranoia is what all of us have. Black people suffer from persecution because real persecution has existed.

G   Yes.

W   White people suffer from a God complex because they have educated themselves to believe they are God.

G   And we have given them a lot of room.

W   And they are paranoid.

G   Because they know that they would not take it.

W   What we have taken.

G   That's right. They know that it has to come back.

W   I'm afraid that black people are going to be pushed into a corner and provoked to real street violence. I truly believe that. And I know that street violence is no good for us. I know that street violence is not going to be our answer. The possibilities of what they intend to do to the minds and the bodies of the men in the prisons . . . they've already started that.

G   Yes.

W   They tried the love gas on the children. They have all these new medical things they're talking about—operations and surgery on the criminal. They want to deal with retarded children. They want to sterilize the woman, they want birth control for all of us, they've got everything planned to destroy us. Now, as I say, there's the law of compensation in the world. It's just as universal as it can be. They cannot destroy everybody without destroying some of themselves.

G   Listen, do you realize that in order to keep one Jonathan Jackson, a seventeen-year-old boy, from escaping with one judge and a couple of guards here or there . . .

W   They would kill 'em all.

G   They killed that judge. And what did they do in Chicago? They have no objections to sacrificing some of themselves.

W   Did you hear about what that man in New Orleans said the other day, that governor of Louisiana? When they asked him if he valued anything more than human life, he said that he valued constituted authority more than human life. That man made that remark.

G   What did Nixon say when the kids at Kent State were killed? Who they knew had no guns, who they knew had to be white?

W   They were bums.

G   They were bums and if they want to fight we'll fight 'em. Knowing that those kids had no guns and that they were their own children. I'm not talking about *my* children.

W   Well, let me tell you. He didn't begin to do any worse at Kent than he did in Washington in May of '71. I was right there and saw it—when they beat all their heads and put them all in jail and they weren't blacks.

G   You can say I'm a child of the twenty-first century, but I don't care whether in order to kill twenty-five million black people they have to kill twenty-five million whites also.

W They don't care.

G   If there are one hundred-and-eighty million of them, that will leave one hundred and fifty-five million white people to no blacks. Right?

W But you see I believe positively that, instead of letting them kill us off, we've got to come to power. I believe that more of us are moving into the thing everyday and yet I don't feel that the mainstream in integration will be the answer until something else more violent happens. I'm afraid of that violence. I don't advocate that violence but I'm afraid it's going to happen. In fact, I think everyday we're looking at it.

G   Of course we're looking at it. I just think that black people have decisions to make about how they are going to respond.

W I think the first thing that's important is education.

G   I won't argue. But I think the first thing is purpose.

W Knowing what you want is what you think is important?

G   We must decide what we want.

W I think that black people can be as ruthless and vicious, once they get any control, as whites.

G What we have to worry about is that we won't get any control.

W I think the answer to getting control is a coalition of people since this is a pluralistic society. There are many different peoples. I think that everybody is going to have to stand up and say, "Well I want my part of it. My share of the pie. I'm not going to take the whole pie because I can't take the whole pie. But I mean to have my share."

G I say *purpose*, which is a term I share with the militants in that we as a people must make a decision based on the fact that we're not pure.

W And not afraid to kill?

G No, don't put words in my mouth.

W All right.

G Is that we're not pure. We as black people have traded in on our so-called innocence: that we are not responsible for the mess we see in America.

W But we are.

G We are, indeed. If we could accept the responsibility that we share. . . .

W Guilt.

G The guilt—O.K., if you want to use that—the guilt that we share for the condition of the world, then we will become responsible enough to move into power. But as long as we play games telling ourselves we're innocent and we've been abused, it's not going to work. Once we can say we are responsible for it, we can begin to formulate the purpose of what we're going to do.

W Don't you think a lot of what has happened to us really is what the white man has done to us?

G No. It takes two people to make a slave: a master and slave. Take it or leave it. The Indians fought and lost but at least they did not surrender, you know what I mean? The Vietnamese fought and they won, so they are free.

W That's not the first time they won, either. They won in 1954 when they got those French out of there.

G I'm just talking in terms of the American context. We are a part of the guilt of this system. And that's one thing that black people are going to have to accept. We cannot escape to Africa, we can't. No more than white folks can escape to the moon. We must deal with what we have here.

W You know, I think we're closer to the real conflict than anyone would imagine? I don't think we're going to go through this decade and come out with the same sort of plain stuff hitting the fan like we did in the sixties.

G But it goes back to those young men that upset you so earlier, like the Essexes. They are taking responsibility. They're saying, "I will not go for it. I will be killed . . ."

W And that's why I don't believe that they're going to bring all those fellows back from Vietnam because of what that war has done to the minds of the black man. It's put some steel and iron in the minds and the backbones of all the black men. Tell me, Nikki, how do you view the future of black people in this country?

G I am concerned because too many black people seem to think that somehow the world . . .

W Ought to be handed to them on a platter.

G If we sit long enough . . .

W And wait, the good Lord will drop it in our laps.

G It won't work and it's not working. And it goes back to what we were talking about earlier. That's why I appreciate at least a response because we know that we cannot hold back the world. It would be a very different world if Africa had conquered Europe rather than Europe conquering Africa. It would be a very different world. But for some reason, despite all of our knowledge, despite all of our technology, despite all of the golden ages of Africa, we never really bothered to go much beyond the Mediterranean Sea. Hannibal would go into Rome because they got tired of coming.

W Well, I'll tell you one thing. When you study Roman history, government and literature, the thing that upsets me (and I couldn't stand that little old woman who taught Latin in Iowa, who was determined that I should never pass because she said I just didn't have the mind to get through it) was what she was always preaching in the Cicero classes: "Remember, Carthage must be destroyed." I don't care if Cicero was talking about the weather or if he was talking about money, he would end by saying, "And remember, Carthage must be destroyed." What was Carthage? A great African city. The culture of Africa declined from the day Rome conquered Carthage and sowed salt.

G So that nothing would grow.

W "Remember and remember," he said, "Carthage must be destroyed." In other words, Rome can never conquer the world until they get rid of those Africans, until they get rid of those black people.

G Of course. But you have the same situation, Margaret, which is what we're talking about, when we deal with America today. We have someone who is determined—I just keep coming back to our current argument because I think it's kind of important. We have an administration . . .

W Determined to destroy us.

G Determined. So determined to destroy us that at this point they don't have to say, "And remember, go get a nigger today." Carthage thought that they could coexist with Rome. They did, they really did, look at it. They said, O.K. Hannibal will go in and we'll show you and then we'll make peace. But the Romans had every intention always of doing exactly what they did. There was to be no peace with Africa. It was to be divided and destroyed and the white man recognized he could not conquer it; he did not have the men or the means to conquer, so he divided it. He got rid of Carthage immediately. But as you come into the New World they used the old tribal priest against us, and we never have understood that tactic.

W Octavius went up there and courted Cleopatra and they destroyed her by her weakness of falling in love with Anthony.

G I never believed that she fell in love. I think she did the best she could, having absolutely no help. Her priests were corrupt, everything around that poor lady was against her; she had no support. Look at it! Some brother told me that one day, "Well, if Cleopatra hadn't fallen in love." I said you gotta be crazy. Nobody was backing her up. Nobody.

W She killed herself because she saw it was hopeless.

G She saw there was nothing more she could do for her people.

W And she wasn't going to Rome to be carried back.

G What happened, I think, to the Egyptians was that they kept knowledge from people and were destroyed. Everyone will pay for trying to hold back a coming age. And certainly if any group of priests were corrupt, the first group that I could put my hands on very easily are the Egyptian priests who had knowledge and said we must keep it for ourselves.

W They understood astrology, they understood philosophy, they understood navigation, they understood mathematics—

G Everything. They refused to give that to their people. Then come to the Roman Church and there is a parallel, which is one reason that you had a Reformation. When the Roman Church would not give the knowledge to the people, the people had to get rid of the church. You come into America, they say we will have education for everybody. As long as they attempted to educate the people you had a strong nation. When they said you cannot educate the slaves, through the black laws, is where I would document the fall of America.

W The trouble with America began with their attitude toward the Indian.

G No, you can't say that because the Indians and the whites fought it out, and the Indians lost. And *all* of us will pay for that, because you always pay for those you hurt. But I'm not going to fight the Indian battle. When you talk about the decline of America, you can take it right back to the

1860s when they said those people are here, they are free, but we will not treat them as men.

W   Well, I think it starts with the very beginning of the country.

G   No, you can't say that, Margaret. You can't say that when a baby is born, he's wrong.

W   The thing that we have to see is what neither black nor white people want to face: that in this country we have developed and arrived at a point where our culture is neither black nor white but mulatto, a synthesis of the two. The white man and the black man are still fighting over their racial integrity or entity when it doesn't exist anymore. It's a terrible thing to say, but I have just as many white ancestors as I've got black. That as an American, I am no pure-blooded African. I am no pure-blooded European. I have ancestors who came from both continents. And the white man doesn't want to admit it but he's got colored folks who are kin to him, just like he's got white folks kin to him. You can't go to the South without finding that this is true. And what America has to face, whether we like it or not, is we've been fighting bitterly trying to destroy the other one, when we're kin to each other.

G   But that's the white man's battle. That is a white man's battle to tell me that he's kin to me.

W   You don't want to hear it, do you?

G   All I'm saying is that we must get in a position that a Faulkner comes up and says I'm kin to Nikki Giovanni. It is not up to me to say I'm kin to a Bill Faulkner.
  If anything has been positive in American history it's that we can say we accept Africa. Africa will be a bit freer, just maybe a bit, when *it* can say we accept Afro-Americans,

because Africans are trying to deny their complicity to our being here.

W I said once that I thought that if Africa had power in the twenty-first century, it would raise the standard and the stature of every black person in the world. That it would be the same as Israel is for the Jew. But that's a long dream away.

G You have to do it country by country.

W That's a long dream away.

G I don't think it's that far away.

W I'm going to say something that is just as negative as it can be. I don't care how great Africa becomes and what her international presence may be, it may raise our stature, but our destiny in America is tied up in America, not just with Africa, because of that twoness and that division in us that Du Bois was always talking about.

G Where is our dilemma? For a Du Bois, or maybe for you, there is a dilemma. It is not a dilemma for me. For me, and I think for a lot of young black people today, it is no longer a dilemma who we are. Our twoness cannot possibly get in the way and that's why these young men can go around and shoot cops. I know you say they're shooting black cops and white cops but they all wear blue. And what they're saying is that the old order must go and be replaced by not only some theoretical choice, but also by a physical choice. That we are saying today, I think quite clearly, that we want humane black people in positions. And we would like to have humane white people work with us. The NAACP can no longer be run by liberal whites. It must be run by black people in conjunction with liberal whites.

W I think that we're getting into a bag there again. Because this is what is happening to us now. We backed up into this bag and it's a literary bag that we're backed up in, and a social bag and an economic bag. This is against what I have said and what I have written. It may be what we feel emotionally, but intellectually I have to question it, and this is why. As long as this country exists, until such time as the black man is standing up in all the halls of government, making all the laws, holding all the money, running all the businesses, there's no such thing as black people having power off by themselves. How do we get power? You're not saying seize it. I contend that the way to recognition and power is not backing off in the black bag entirely and saying that we can do everything by ourselves, we don't need these people and the best thing we can do is not to let them run our situations. You're saying let's get in our separatist bag, and separate.

G I did not say that.

W You said if we have black organizations, don't let the white man run it.

G I said he can't *run* it. Margaret, you didn't hear me at all.

W You did say get him out.

G We can play the tape back if you want to hear it.

W What did you say?

G I said that in terms of power, we must assume it.

W How? Tell me how.

G You know what assume means?

W *(impatiently)* Yeah, yeah.

G O.K., we must prepare ourselves and assume it.

W To take over from the white man?

G The problem is that black people don't want to take re-sponsibility for white people, and that includes, if I may say, you. We have simply got to say, this is what we're gonna do, this is how we're gonna do it and this is what you must do to make it work. Because white people have shown that they are not capable of taking responsibility for either them-selves or us. And they've had every chance in the world to do it. It is now time for *us* to assume that role. We are the rightful heirs. That's all I'm saying. I'm not saying that we have to kill them off, I didn't say that we have to go and take the state of Mississippi over and live by ourselves; that's foolish. What we must do, what we must do if this country is to survive in any kind of political entity as we now know it is to take—

W We've got to have a truce, haven't we?

G But we have got to control it. You cannot take any cracker's word. How can you take Nixon's word? If we walk out in the street today, if we walk out on the Senate floor, half the senators don't believe in Nixon's cease-fire.

W I just think you need about two years—

G For what? In two years you and I won't be able to sit here without some guard standing there if we continue to let the Nixons run this country. We've got to continue moving and we've got to make a decision that we don't mind controlling white people.

W We're already moving toward fascism. We're already into fascism.

G That's what black people don't want to do and that's what our problem is: We don't want to make a decision for those white folks. And we have got to do that and it's got to be shown in our literature. We cannot, you know, today still write stereotypical white people; it will not suffice. It will not suffice that we try to deal with them in the kind of way—what's that play LeRoi wrote, where they're all sitting around looking at TV and we laugh at them—we have got to be better. And that's an awful thing to say to a people who are much less on a certain scale. We have simply got to be better. For our own sanity.

W Well, aren't we already?

G *(emphatically)* No. No. No.

W We've got to get the skills.

G We've got to do what they do . . .

W Better.

G Better. If we can do what they do as well as what we do, we will be better. Because they're not trying to learn how to learn what we do. They send them little white boys to grow their hair, to try to sing them songs, they try to say if you get rid of niggers at least I'll be here to sing the blues. And blacks have got to say if we get rid of white people at least I'll be here to govern! But we want to say, well I can sing and dance, fuck that. What else can you do?

W The answer is in understanding how that political, imperial, financial, military business works and cracking it up.

G   But it ain't no secret.

W   You know how it works?

G   It ain't no secret. I can sit on the Senate floor and vote for my friends to get a milk bill through and I can be President and let my secretary bug Watergate. I can do that. The point is that it's just one of me, you understand what I mean? We need a hundred blacks sitting there saying, "Well I can do that." That ain't no secret. What it takes is discipline. What it takes is that you get up at eight in the morning and you call John and say, John we got this bill, it's got to be passed, man. You got to help me out. Well, I'll give you my vote if you give me his vote, but what we want to do is wake up at noon, you understand what I mean? We've got to start getting up when dawn breaks and go to bed at midnight with no complaints.

W   As my grandmother used to say, while they're asleep you've got to be thinking how you can beat them.

G   You know, it's the world we're talking about. . . .